UNDER THE BLACK BULL'S HOOVES

Under the *Black Bull's* HOOVES

Histories of the Camargue

Maritta Kaumanns

SilverWood

Published in 2023 by SilverWood Books

SilverWood Books Ltd
14 Small Street, Bristol, BS1 1DE, United Kingdom
www.silverwoodbooks.co.uk

Text copyright © Maritta Kaumanns 2023
Photographs copyright © Maritta Kaumanns 2023 unless otherwise stated
Photographs on page 12 © Archive Muscat
Logo copyright © Fiona Richmond

The right of Maritta Kaumanns to be identified as the author of this
work has been asserted in accordance with the Copyright,
Designs and Patents Act 1988 Sections 77 and 78.

All rights reserved. No part of this publication may be reproduced,
stored in a retrieval system, or transmitted in any form or by any means,
electronic, mechanical, photocopying, recording or otherwise,
without prior permission of the copyright holder.

ISBN 978-1-80042-239-1 (paperback)

British Library Cataloguing in Publication Data
A CIP catalogue record for this book is
available from the British Library

To Annie and Henri Laurent

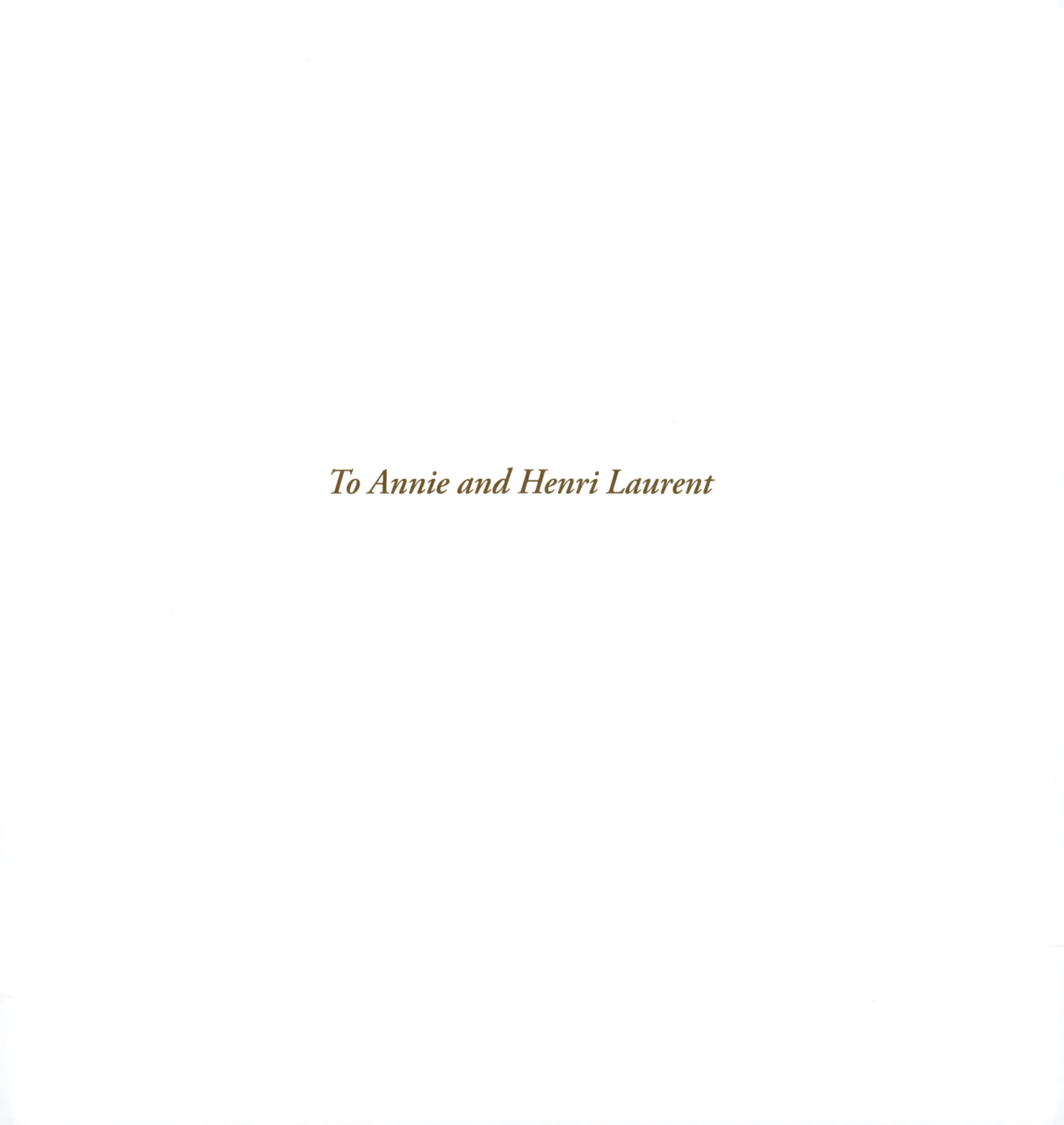

Contents

Preface 9

Chapter 1: **A Bull Called Goya** 13

Chapter 2: **The Pilgrimage** 29

Chapter 3: **Phoenix Rises From The Ashes** 49

Chapter 4: **The Mad Marquis** 69

Chapter 5: **The Stoicism of the Herdsman** 91

Chapter 6: **The Camargue Horse** 111

Chapter 7: **Under the Black Bull's Hooves** 133

Chapter 8: **The Loyalty Factor** 155

Epilogue 177

Appendix and Sources 181

Preface

Falling in love with a wild Camargue bull has consequences. Most Provence travellers know of the white horses and the flamingos of the Camargue and they may notice black bulls grazing in the distance. Few know that these bulls are the beating heart of the Camargue. They are a unique species that doesn't exist anywhere else in the world and they have an equally unique task: they perform in French bull games, have done so for nearly 1000 years. No harm is done to them and the bull always wins. Without them the Camargue with its abundance of fauna and flora wouldn't exist.

    In the seventies I went to a competition and found myself totally smitten by a spectacular animal called Goya. The aim of the game is for young men to pick ribbons tied between the horns of the bull and they risk their lives doing so. Goya proved to be a true star with character. He clearly enjoyed chasing his opponents at rocket speed, jumping over six-foot-high barricades and walls in hot pursuit. He even interacted with an audience terrified and delighted in equal measure.

A passion was born, but I had to wait nearly four decades to return and explore what turned out to be an eccentric regional niche culture, unknown beyond the Camargue. For many centuries this culture's poetry and novels, songs, festive traditions and even politics have had the cult of the bull at their centre. I discovered that the people are like a tribe, jealously guarding the soul of their universe – tourists are generally welcome but prying eyes are not. Privileged to befriend Goya's charismatic owners, a veritable dynasty of the Camargue, I embarked on a journey into the mythical world of wild bulls that cannot be tamed, have a mind of their own and often exceptional longevity. Like an apprentice, I gradually learned how these extremely intelligent, agile animals with their individually distinct personalities live and are cared for. I gained knowledge about the true role of the legendary Camargue horse. Gradually I found access to a fascinating system of unwritten laws and sophisticated, ancient rituals. Anecdotes I heard and events I witnessed ranged from tragic to comical to heroic and never lacked drama.

Under the Black Bull's Hooves is their story. It is an invitation to catch a glimpse of the fiery, often quirky souls of men and beasts alike, their history and their skills, the sadness and the joy of individual events. It is a declaration of love to the last coastal wilderness in Europe and the people whose lives are dedicated to nature and the preservation of its fragile balance.

Opposite: Goya 1978 (Archive Laurent)

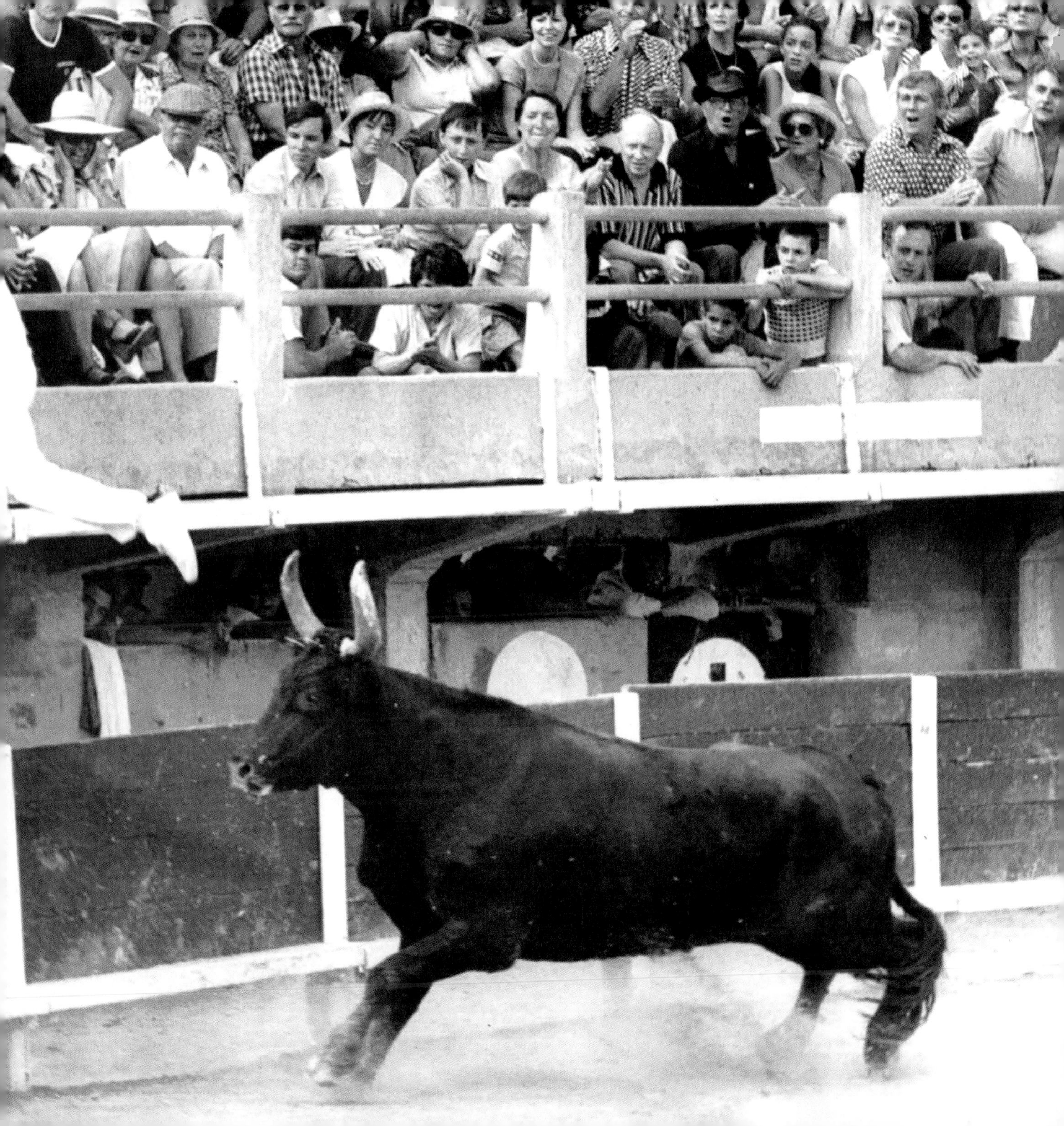

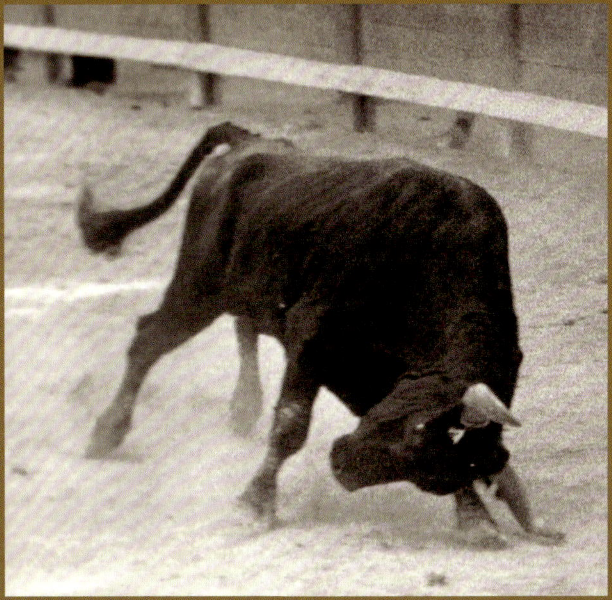
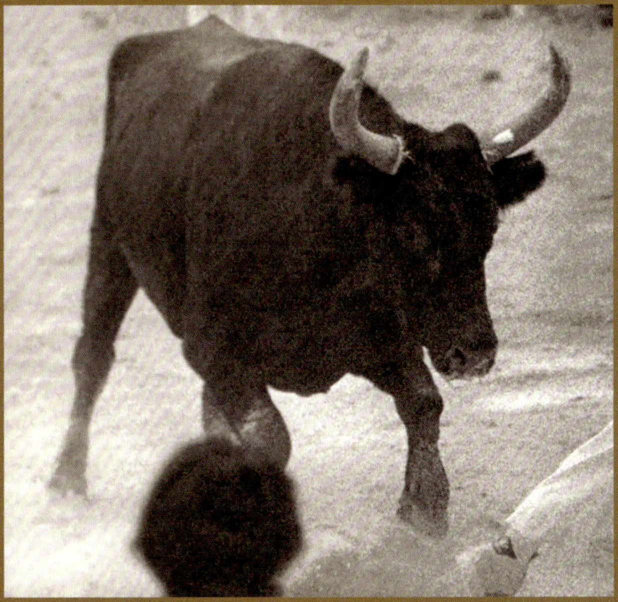

Chapter 1

A Bull Called Goya

Corrida – it screamed, from huge posters on walls, in shop windows, on doors. The artistically perfect, colourful images advertising Spanish bullfights tainted my picture of a light-flooded, relaxed and peaceful Provence. Killing bulls did not fit this ideal. As a young journalist, working in the cultural department of a German daily newspaper, I was on holiday in the south of France, looking for beauty and a slower pace of life. In the early 1970s the Côte d'Azur was already clogged up by mass tourism and I had quickly fled west, leaving time to explore the timeless mix of ancient Roman and modern French flair around Nimes, Arles and the Camargue.

I didn't know that Spanish bullfights were allowed in the south of France and I couldn't escape the seemingly ubiquitous depictions of this archaic ritual sacrificing of magnificent animals for entertainment.

Then I noticed other, smaller posters, depicting men clad in white touching the head of a black bull in full flight. These ones advertised *Course Camarguaise*, French bullfighting. It looked more like an exciting game that didn't seem to hurt the bull.

The grumpy owner of my favourite bar in Arles took three seconds of his precious time to explain the difference between the two. After slamming a double espresso on my table he stood tall, expanding his chest to the fullest.

'*Corrida* celebrates death. *Courses Camarguaises* celebrate life!' he declaimed.

Before I could ask any further questions, he added that it was too complicated to explain it all to a tourist. I would have to see for myself.

Two days later I sat in the packed arena of a small town. There was a prelude: trumpets, an orchestra playing the *Toreador* tune from Bizet's *Carmen*, radiant young Provençale women dressed in traditional *Arlésienne* costumes crossing the sand of the oval and, finally, a formation of young men in white saluting the audience. They were called *raseteurs*, ready to take on the six bulls named on the leaflet I had received together with my ticket.

Moments later the first bull entered the arena. His glistening black coat reflected the sun. He wasn't that tall but he had a lean, muscled frame. Mighty horns pointing skywards demanded respect. Between the horns he carried pieces of cotton – a small red one in the middle called *cocarde*, two white tassels near the ears and rounds of string at the base of his horns. Calmly he inspected the arena while the men in white chinos and T-shirts observed him from the aisle between the red planks limiting the ring and the wall. On the blast of a trumpet they all jumped in, circling the bull as if to find the best place to pick off his trophies with a little iron claw, a *crochet*, in their hand.

Opposite: Black bulls grazing in total freedom

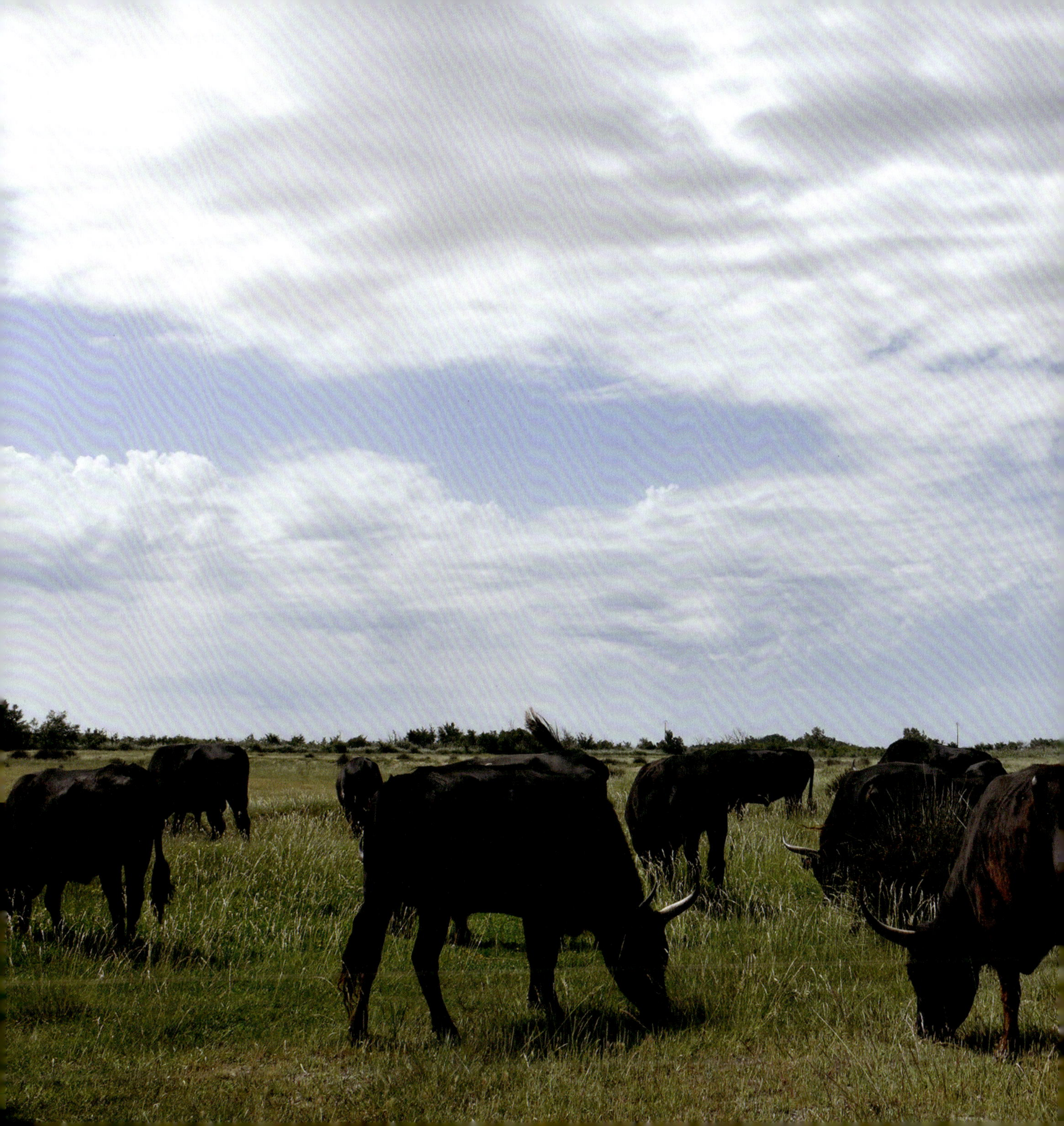

The bull had other ideas. Frequently changing position, his vivid eyes constantly swivelling to guard himself against any sign of attack, he was determined to defend his crown. White and black would certainly not run towards each other like longing lovers. Suddenly a *raseteur* went for it. Running across the bull's eyeline at a short distance, he invited him to a chase. Four legs accelerated like a racing car, soon catching up with the opponent. For a brief moment a hand rested on the bull's head trying to detach the red *cocarde* before the young man had to run for his life. Just in time he jumped over the barricade to hang on to the metal rails on top of the wall, separating the audience from the action below.

A sequence of close encounters unfolded. I noticed that the *cocarde* and the two tassels were held by rubber bands and seemed easier to grab than the strings around the base of the horns. The *raseteurs* had to risk more to detach these as it required numerous dangerous attempts. Shrieks of fear from the audience erupted each time the bull's horns came near enough to pierce his opponent's body but that was the thrill they all had come to experience. Each spectacular action was accompanied by fanfares from *Carmen*, rewarding the men as well as the animal. After fifteen minutes the sound of the trumpet signalled the end of the competition. With his head held high and the strings left to carry home the bull trotted towards the *toril*, his exit gate.

Two more bulls appeared, each one more agile, more aggressive and powerful than the last. Then there was an interval.

I sat next to a local couple who had come armed with parasols and cushions to sit on. Even during the most dangerous moments they didn't bat an eyelid, only nodding approvingly every now and then. I asked them why the names of the animals were printed in larger letters on the posters than those of the *raseteurs*.

'That's because the bulls are the stars,' they replied.

I wanted to know if there were any rules. They seemed surprised that a foreigner needed details on what, to them, seemed an entirely private affair.

'Yes, a lot of rules. It's far too complicated to explain. As a tourist you wouldn't understand.' Firmly put in my place for the second time I felt as if I'd gatecrashed a wedding party.

After the interval a bull called Goya was announced and all hell broke loose. The gate opened but this animal didn't simply enter the arena – he danced into it. Hundreds of people jumped to their feet, greeting him with applause, shouting his name in a frenzied rhythm. Fast and light-footed, Goya trotted a full round, accepting the honours while already sizing up the *raseteurs* waiting behind the bright red barricades, ducking out of his sight the moment he came near the planks. The trumpet sounded but there was no rush to arrange close encounters with Goya. Minutes passed in total silence. People started whistling and hurling insults at the whites. Finally, one had courage enough make a dash but stayed well clear of Goya's head. Another one had a more decisive go. With lightning speed Goya closed in, caught hold of him and whipped him up into the air like a doll. He fell to the ground and tried to crawl towards the saving barricade, expecting the worst. Nobody could help; they could only try to distract the bull, coax him away from his victim. There was no need – as if he had made his point Goya left him in peace to be recovered by medics.

Only then did I realise that there was an ambulance on stand-by. Minutes later this ambulance got very busy. For the moment there were no further opponents to deal with and Goya grew bored. Standing near the planks, he stared at the empty sands, impatiently scratching the ground with his front hooves. All of a sudden he crossed the chest-

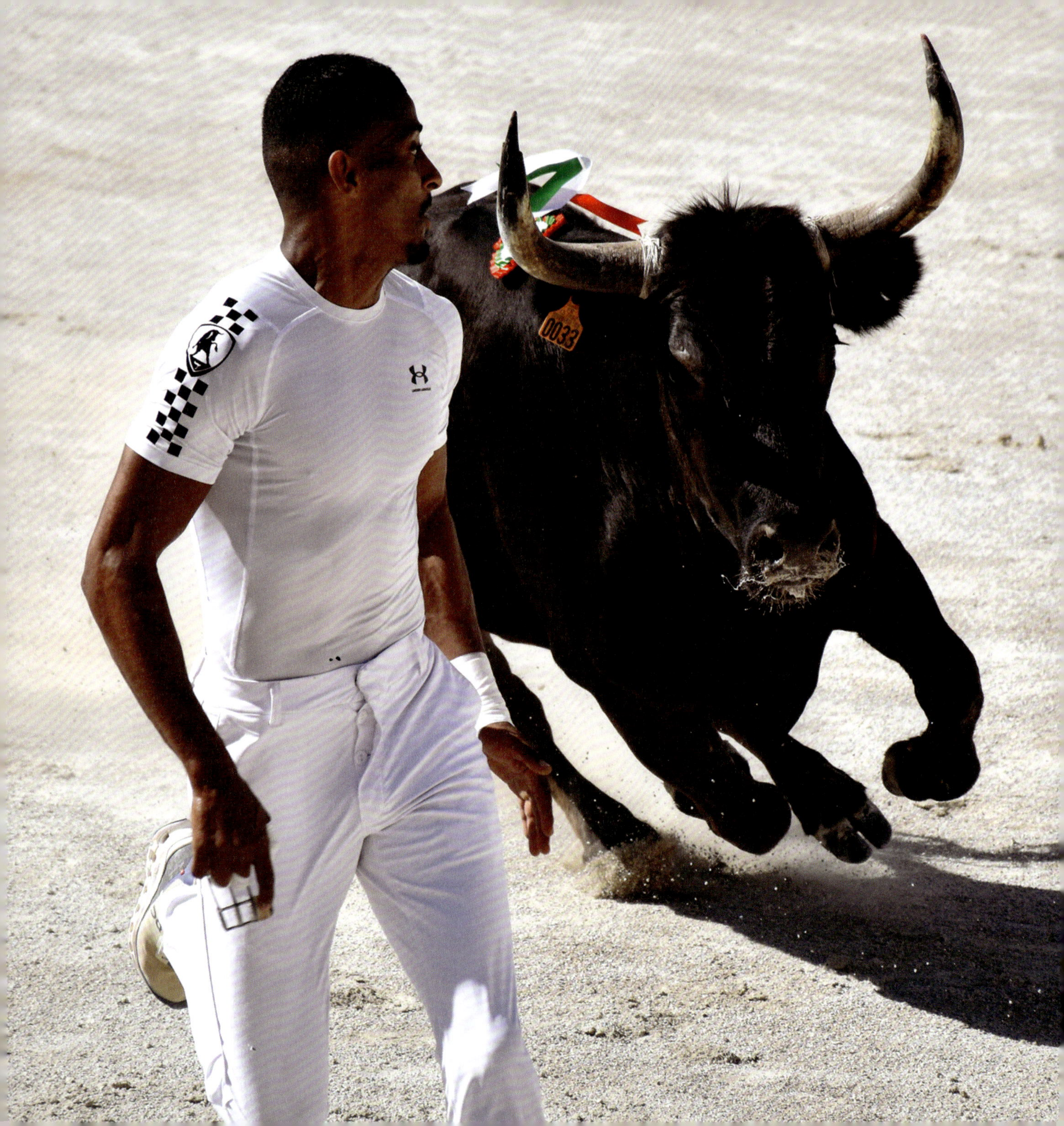
0033

high barrier with an elegant jump and went for the spectators crowding the aisle, hoovering them up one by one. Anybody not fast enough to jump over the planks was swiftly tossed into the arena. Enjoying the panic he had caused, Goya looked at an empty aisle and I was sure I could see a grin on his face. With the same ease he jumped back into the ring to have more fun. There was no way any of the bits decorating his head would be picked off in the ongoing chaos. Dozens of people ran in every direction, often in vain, to flee the sharply pointed horns as more than a thousand others cheered Goya on. Dominating a by now empty oval, his interest turned to demolishing the barricades. When the trumpet finally sounded, he stopped cold, pivoted and left in the same way he had entered – dancing home to thunderous applause, accompanied by an ear-shattering sequence of Carmen's *Les Toreadors*. He wasn't even out of breath.

I was totally smitten by this deity called Goya and his brothers. The animals were neither taunted nor harmed in any way and they seemed to enjoy chasing people. Who owned these intelligent beasts? How did they live?

A few days later I set off to explore their home, the Camargue. This southern extension of Provençe, bordering on the Mediterranean, is a delta formed by two mighty branches of the river Rhône, extending westwards into the Languedoc. On the map it looks like a large triangle approaching Montpellier to the west, bordering Arles in the north and the massive refineries of Fos-sur-Mer in the East encroaching on rural peace. Only recently, in 1970, had this region been put under protection. The newly created regional park covered 100,000 hectares.

The light of Provençe has attracted artists for centuries. I entered the Camargue south of Arles where this light seemed even more intense, more glaring. Farmed land gave way to open plains

Opposite: A raseteur running for his life

Goya on the heels of Muscat (Archive Muscat)

and watery prairies. It was sparsely settled but now, in mid-spring, the main roads were busy with tourists trying to fight off billions of mosquitos while looking for flamingos and more than 400 other bird species populating the marshes and lagoons. The famous white horses were attractive too: dozens of ranches lined the main route to Saintes-Maries-de-la-Mer, offering short excursions. I saw hundreds of horses saddled up and looking decidedly bored while waiting to carry riders of varying experience.

Nobody was looking for bulls but then – there were no bulls to be seen anywhere. I went off the main roads, ambling along small lanes and dirt tracks. The view was endless; sky and earth seemed to merge into one. Approaching a small forest I noticed huge birds' nests in its trees and I stopped to look up. It was a large colony of storks. I hadn't seen those since my early childhood in Germany. Lost in awe and wonder, I lingered to watch majestic adults flying in and out of nests, providing an endless chain of food for their offspring.

All of a sudden sinister cloud formations darkened the sky, chased by the infamous *Mistral* wind whistling down the Rhône valley. Within seconds, blistering heat changed into an icy chill. The *Mistral* can blow for minutes or several weeks. In the latter case it is said to drive even the most balanced soul into madness. This was a harsh climate but it was magic too and I felt deeply touched by the drama the heavens offered. Nowhere could one be closer to nature; nowhere else could have demonstrated better how insignificant our small lives can be.

Half an hour later the weather changed back to calmness and warmth. Unexpectedly a small herd of black bulls appeared, grazing their way around the trees. Only a fence separated me from them. They looked up, alerted by my presence. Sharp eyes scrutinised me, weighing up if I represented a danger or not. All of them looked athletic, with slim hips and broad chests. Large goblet- or lyre-shaped horns pointed straight upwards. After a few minutes they decided that I was harmless and turned back to nibbling herbs. These creatures were wild and graceful – no wonder that the god of sky and thunder, Zeus, had to turn himself into a bull to seduce Europa. No wonder that they had been perceived as gods for thousands of years.

French bull games were the modern version of ancient cults, leaving the animals alive and well looked after. A sense of professional duty should have compelled me to continue visiting museums, art galleries and theatre performances, but the pull of the bulls was too strong and I carried on looking for the *Courses Camarguaises*.

I saw Goya in action again in a small arena with little separation between the ring and the spectators. Jumping all barriers as usual, he climbed the ranks to sow delightful panic. Roles were reversed – half the audience was assembled inside the arena while a triumphant Goya stood, one leg cocked, on top of the seats, waiting a few moments before jumping back on to the sand to create more mayhem.

Desperate to find out more, I went to a bookshop, hoping for some literature on what was clearly a unique culture. This kind of bull game didn't exist anywhere else in the world but there were no books to be found. A shopkeeper pointed me towards a magazine, published monthly. The *Camariguo* contained forty pages packed with photos, articles and reports on all bullfights in the region. Devouring the magazine at night, I felt like I was reading quality theatre reviews, written with care and passion, though some were in Provençal, the regional language which I couldn't understand. Nonetheless, the magazine allowed me to catch a glimpse of a complicated system of competition rules and insights into a tradition that expressed a deeply rooted love for bulls in novels, poetry and music.

One name appeared on nearly every page: Laurent. The Laurent family owned Goya and many more champions. They seemed to be the dominant dynasty among the ranchers, called *manadiers*, in the Camargue, contributing to a revival of the ancient tradition of the *Courses Camarguaises* from 1944 onwards. They had their opponents, though, as became obvious the more I read. Readers' comments revealed a hot discussion revolving around Goya and his qualities as a fighter. There were those who claimed he was not a proper, traditional bull because of his love for jumping the barricades and interacting with the audience. Others admired Goya's intelligence, his style and the way he outwitted the *raseteurs* who tried in vain to deprive him of his little cotton accolades. Many saw him as a symbol of the youth rebellion that had begun in the 1960s, breathing fresh air into a stale society and attitudes frozen in the past. I instantly sided with the latter faction.

The magazine also listed upcoming events, among them one of

The art of snatching a ribbon

the biggest annual competitions in the Roman arena of Arles. The six best bulls of the year so far, including Goya, would appear.

On the day of the contest I left early in the morning only to find a long queue in front of the ticket counters. They closed at 11am; all tickets were sold out. The festivities would begin at 4pm. The streets around the arena were filled with trucks transporting horses and bulls, accompanied by *gardians* – the French version of a cowboy.

Together with hundreds of others I stayed on the large plaza in front of the main entrance, hoping somebody would give up their ticket. The sun bore down fiercely but most of us didn't budge. With longing eyes I saw locals and tourists entering, tickets in hand. At 2pm all doors closed, locking in 15,000 people waiting to see Goya. At 4pm the first tunes of Bizet's *Carmen* signalled the opening ceremonies. Alone on the suddenly deserted plaza, I slumped on a Roman pillar stump, unable to hold back tears. Moments later I felt a shadow over my head. A lean, middle-aged man bent down.

'What's wrong, my lovely one?' he asked.

His weathered face had a kind smile. He wore traditional Camargue moleskin trousers, a colourful shirt and scuffed boots. Between sobs I told him about my despair of not being able to see Goya. He took my face between his hands. They felt rough, firm and warm.

Staring at strings of white horsehair on his trousers I asked, 'Are you a *gardian*?'

He nodded. 'Come with me,' he said, took my hand and pulled me up. We went around the arena to enter a massive entrance tunnel. Through the darkness he led me to a spot on top of the arch above the *toril*, once the entrance for Roman gladiators but, these days, for bulls and their opponents.

'Sit here. Best place in the entire arena,' he said and left before I could thank him.

For over four hours I witnessed a feast of music, dancing horses and Provençal ceremonies followed by the thrilling scenes of four-legged blacks and two-legged whites trying to outwit each other. Thousands groaned and screamed during moments of utmost danger, applauded bulls and *raseteurs* for every spectacular action, and all rose to their feet as one when the emperor of the Camargue, Goya, entered the ring. He didn't disappoint – the ambulances on stand-by soon filled up. His attacks were never intentionally vicious. To him this was a game but his horns could kill. On this day they didn't.

We were all transformed into a community of noisy worshippers, completely enthralled by a powerful ritual celebrating life and the beauty of the wild. I began to understand why the locals were reticent to share the mystery of the Camargue. Like an oyster they clammed up whenever a nosy outsider tried to touch the pearl their community guarded.

Opposite: Horses love flowers

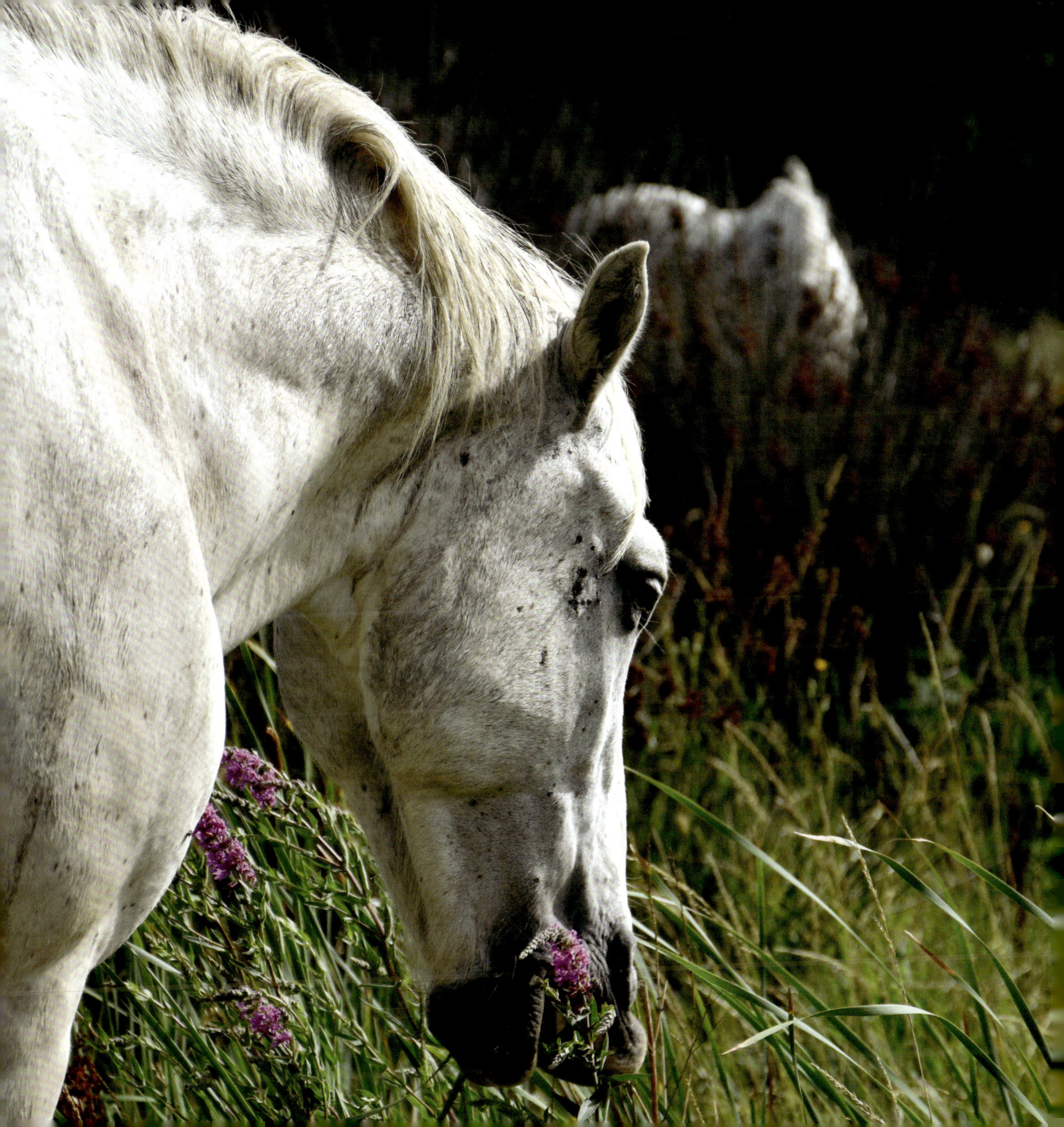

Flamingos in a Camargue lagoon

I would have loved to write an article about these impressive animals but felt that I didn't command enough knowledge to do so. Reluctantly returning to Germany, I swore to myself that, one day, I would have the time to explore the exotic, secluded world of black bulls on the edge of the Mediterranean.

Opposite: 'Are you coming back down to play?'

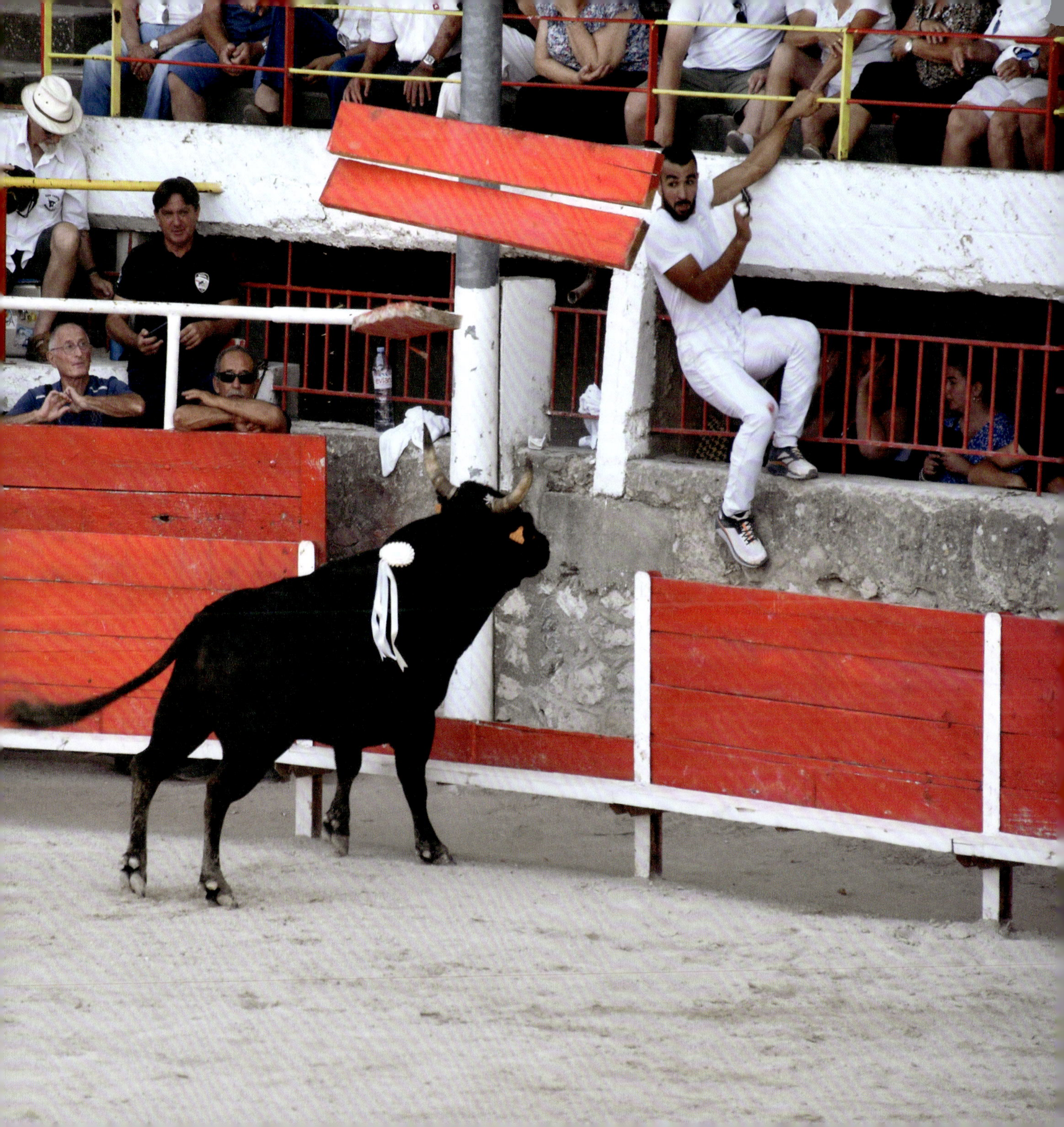

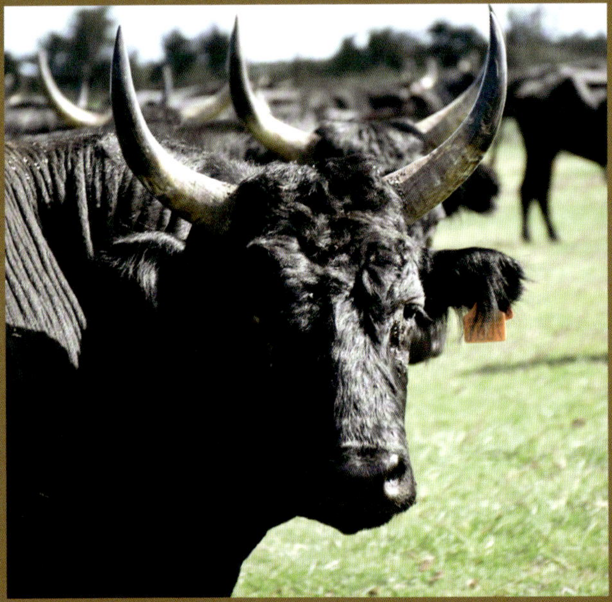
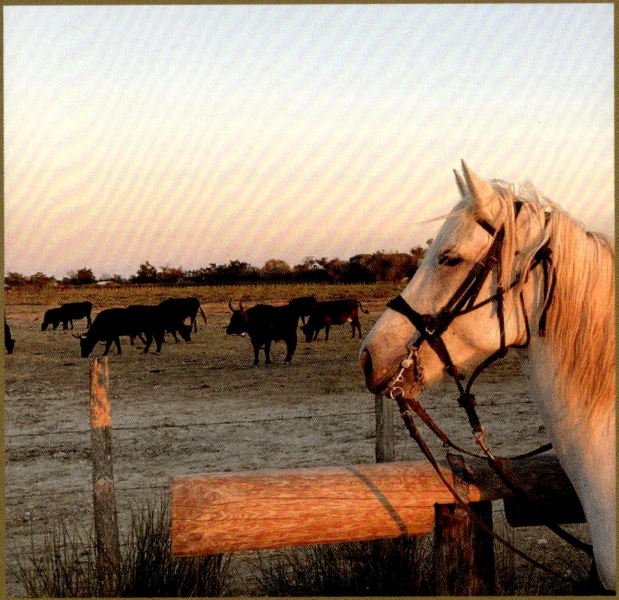

Chapter 2

The Pilgrimage

I didn't see Goya again. Thirty-eight years passed without a single opportunity to return to the Camargue and I nearly forgot about my bullish passion. I had relocated to the UK in the 1990s and, on one of the many drab London winter days in 2013, it dawned on me that I was free, free to go wherever I wanted. My journalistic life had led me from writing theatre and art reviews to foreign affairs, including war coverage. For fifteen years. I had focussed on the Middle East. Love for nature left me deeply impacted by the intensity of its desert landscapes but equally traumatised by covering its numerous, never-ending conflicts. In the end retiring came as a relief, together with a longing for beauty – the beauty of nature.

There were no more family members I had to look after, no professional obligations, no more problems to deal with. None whatsoever.

The view from the windows of my London flat offered skies filled with cold drizzle and slow-moving dark clouds. One of them shifted shape, taking on the contours of a wild black bull. It sent a jolt down my spine. Torrents of memories flooded my brain. I turned to my laptop, hesitantly typing Goya's name and that of his owners, the Laurents, into Google.

He instantly sprang back to life. Grainy videos showed him clearing out entire arenas, happily flicking people high up into the air (often without hurting them) and crowds cheering him on. There was footage of the inauguration of a larger-than-life statue erected in his honour in Beaucaire, the home town of the Laurent family. I saw photos of Goya being hand-fed at home, the bull's eyes dreamy with delight. Goya's biography told of retirement after ten years of wreaking havoc in every arena across the Camargue, winning all available awards along the way. Numerous accounts of *raseteur*s who had, often without success, tried to pick the pieces tied between and around his horns, were full of respect and love for an animal that had left some of them injured and scarred for life albeit without regret.

Resting peacefully at home, Goya seemed to enjoy the frequent visits of admirers. In his old age he made friends with a cow from a neighbouring ranch and they disappeared together, apparently seeking privacy. Strictly speaking he was a steer, castrated like most of his brothers in horns, but out of respect this word is never used. Yet, nobody was surprised that he showed interest in a cow. Efforts to keep him on home ground were soon abandoned. Still effortlessly jumping fences, ditches and hedges to reach his confidante, he spent a lot of time with her. From afar, they were seen cheek to cheek, grazing and wandering around, always "in touch" with each other.

On a cold winter morning in 1986 he was found, seemingly

asleep, in exactly the spot where he had been born twenty-two years earlier. Goya had joined his noble ancestors in the heavenly pantheon of the Camargue.

It is custom to bury famous bulls upright and facing the sea where, as legend has it, they had once come from. This is done in a private ceremony. Goya's grave in the grounds of the Laurent family estate remains deliberately unmarked since other tombs in the Camargue have been raided for souvenirs. However, there is a stone column in Goya's honour near the main building.

The Internet turned out to be an invaluable source of information, a veritable Camargue encyclopedia on everything to do with bulls, their owners, history, legends, ecology and festivities. It all seemed still very alive. I passed countless hours, day and night, in front of the screen, bleary-eyed, gobbling up as much as possible while reviving my French without even noticing it.

Spring was around the corner and probably already in full swing in Provençe. Armed with more knowledge, the desire to connect again with this bovine obsession became irresistible. An old warning rang in my ear:

'Don't try to repeat the happy holidays you had decades ago – everything has changed and you will be disappointed!'

Too late. The car was packed and raring to go.

The first port of call was Beaucaire. Located on a picturesque stretch of the river Rhône, the town had been one of the mightiest and richest trading centres in France until the seventeenth century when changing trade routes caused decline. During the centuries of wealth an annual huge trade fair stretched for miles over the floodplains outside the city walls.

I remembered glancing up at pastel-coloured, flower-decorated walls of palatial houses amidst bustling street life beneath and watching people playing pétanque in the shade of huge plane trees.

Now I was in for a shock. Apart from a few women fully covered in chadors and hijabs hurrying through narrow streets, lined with overflowing rubbish bags, there was hardly any sign of life. Normally southern towns and villages wake up after a long lunchtime break and outdoor activities resume. But Beaucaire remained silent. Here and there human faeces decorated the pavement and the spring air was heavy with the smell of stale urine. A lot of the once proud facades had lost their rendering, revealing big patches of raw brickwork around precariously rusty balconies. The long high street had only a few shops not boarded up, among them a halal butcher, two groceries, a pharmacy and a newspaper shop which also sold tobacco and lottery tickets.

Turn back! I told myself, but the car kept meandering through town until we reached a roundabout. And there, at its centre in the midst of flowerbeds in full bloom, the gleaming white statue of Goya stood glistening in the sun. A tree-lined boulevard led down to a canal connecting the Rhône and the fishing port of Sète in the Languedoc. The restaurants and bars along the waterline were busy, boats swayed gently on their moorings – there was still life in the old town after all.

A few days later I sat in the reasonably filled large arena of Beaucaire, named after Paul Laurent, founder of the Laurent dynasty. Armed with newly gained knowledge, I had a better understanding of the performance of both bulls and *raseteurs*. Outside there were stalls selling bull pottery, bull pictures, belts adorned with tiny brass bull horns and bull glasses. I bought one with Goya's head on it, casually mentioning that I had "known" him. It worked like a magic password. People, especially younger ones, were surprised at a foreigner with an interest in bulls, asking me what Goya had really been like. Soon

Goya's monument in Beaucaire

animated conversations about the current state of affairs in the bull world stretched over an hour, further enlivened by a few rounds of *pastis*. The Laurents and other ranchers were still a force to be reckoned with but overall, I heard, nothing could compare to past glories. The *raseteurs* didn't respect the bulls enough; they were not as engaged as in the past. The bulls were not as powerful or intelligent or aggressive as they used to be and on it went. Typically Provençal, I thought, but they were right in so far as we hadn't seen anything spectacular.

Hungry for more, I checked a calendar on the Internet listing all *Courses Camarguaises* for the entire season until November. There were more than 850 advertised for all the towns and villages surrounding the Camargue. Traditionally six or seven bulls from different *manades* compete for fifteen minutes each. Hundreds of animals were listed in

Les Marquises – seat of the Manade Laurent

competitions with each other and against the *raseteurs*. *Manade* means "herd" in Provençal but it also means "ranch", the place where they are born and bred, led by the *manadier*, the rancher. I was especially keen on a *Course Camarguaise* in a big arena in Palavas, near Montpellier. The advertised bulls were all owned by the Laurents and would defend the colours – white, green, red – of the Manade Laurent. This was called a *Royale*, giving an individual owner the chance to allow his best animals to perform without rivals from other ranches.

Waiting to finally catch a glimpse of this illustrious dynasty, I revisited all the places that had enthralled me in the 1970s. It turned out to be a time warp. Many towns, among them Arles, hadn't changed much. It looked a bit poorer but then the financial crisis emanating from Wall Street in 2008 had hit home everywhere. The restaurants where still the same and some traditional shops were still in business after eighty years and more. Even the fashion had reverted back to the hippy days. The only difference I could spot was tapered jeans and the preference of young men for shortly cropped hair, leaving just a bit of a hedgehog shape on top of their heads. Mobile phones were in use but people engaged and socialised with each other as before. The powerful voice of Edith Piaf filled the terrace of a bar near the old amphitheatre; elsewhere I heard the songs of Jacques Brel, Charles Aznavour and Julien Clerc wafting through clear spring air. Forty years of rap and more recent pop hadn't left a dent in the popularity of the French eternals. I breathed a deep sigh of relief. It was possible to live a happy past in a modern present.

Delight peaked when I discovered shops stocking a fair amount of books on the Camargue. All of them were written in French. Some consisted mainly of stunning photos appealing to tourists, but there was also a range covering what makes the Camargue tick: biographies of ranchers, individual bulls and books explaining in great detail the art of raising and training the white horses. Some concentrated on the ecology of the Camargue while others told the history of *gardians*, the herdsmen. Several books described the skill required to become a *raseteur* and there were soulful accounts of the deep, nearly spiritual relationship between the Camargue people and their land and its animals. Hardly any of these had existed in the seventies, but now I could even find reprints of books going back to the early twentieth century.

The only fly in the ointment was the amount of new roads cutting through what I remembered as pristine landscape. Admittedly one can't set the past in aspic. Over recent decades the region had become the most prolific grower of organic fruit and vegetables in France. Middle-class soft tourism, another big economic factor in Provence, had grown as well. Both tourism and agriculture required improved infrastructure and the French administration would never

Goya's column at Les Marquises

shy away from forcing through a project they deemed necessary, even if it involves the unceremonious dispossession of private territory without delay.

I swallowed the roads because they had brought prosperity, and with it an improvement in animal welfare, so close to my heart. In the seventies I had seen neglected horses and numerous emaciated stray animals. Now everybody looked well cared for and properly fed – including the owners.

The seaside resort of Palavas, on the western edge of the Camargue near the ever-growing urban sprawl of Montpellier, is a popular destination for mass tourism. Towers and cubes of concrete hotel buildings dwarf the once charming centre of the former fishing village, now lined with tatty souvenir shops and eateries overcrowded by people happy to fry on the beach in the cheapest way possible.

Today the town was invaded by a different kind of visitor: 3000 fans of the *Course Camarguaise* queued up to fill the ranks of the arena. Patiently we applauded the festive prelude, complete with Camargue horse and rider displays and other traditional rituals before, finally, the first black beast entered the sandy oval. They would appear in order of experience and skill and none of them disappointed. Their chosen names – like Cassius, Troubadour, Cyrano and Quo Vadis to list a few – carried hopes and individual characteristics: while Troubadour had a lyrical approach to playfully chasing his opponents beyond the barricades, Cassius was clearly aiming for a direct run and a quick knockout. During the interval there was a flurry of heated exchanges among connoisseurs: 'The Laurent bulls jump too much!' was vehemently contradicted by the true *Laurentistas*: 'No, they don't; they're more aggressive, more intelligent than any others; you're just jealous!'

The competition over, I wondered where the Laurents were, only to find them behind the arena, surrounded by several hundreds of fans and the press. I drew a deep breath seeing them for the first time in person – this was royalty holding court! The seniors, Henri Laurent and his wife Annie, and their son Patrick with his wife Estelle could have come right off a glamorous film set. They looked majestic in their traditional costumes – well-cut moleskin trousers, waistcoats, black velvet jackets and wide-brimmed hats, all individually tailored. Annie wore a splendid green dress typical for *Arlésiennes*, the ladies of Arles. Henri was in especially high demand and I had to join a long queue congratulating him. During decades of journalism I had done many interviews with well-known artists or politicians without any kind of stage fright but now, for the first time, I felt a flurry of butterflies churning my stomach.

Finally it was my turn. Henri Laurent was elderly but the way he carried himself belied his age. A deeply grooved, kind face with an impressive moustache, glints of a mischievous sense of humour and vivid dark-brown eyes looked at me with curiosity. He had instantly recognised me as a foreigner. His handshake had an assuring, firm grip. Lost for words I simply said that I had come from London to see his bulls performing. The face erupted in beams of a radiant smile; he pivoted around and, with a booming voice, announced to the crowds: 'Look, she has come all the way from London to see our *Royale*!'

A warm glow calmed the butterflies in my stomach. Reluctantly I withdrew, making space for other worshippers. I stayed on to observe, noticing after a while that I myself was being watched. Annie Laurent had kept in the background, leaving Henri and the younger family members to absorb the attention. Standing erect like a statue, she seemed to rest within herself, aware of an authority which she wore with ease. Her piercing blue-green eyes had zeroed in on me. After a few minutes of further assessment she approached me.

Annie and Henri Laurent (Archive Laurent)

'I would like to invite you to Les Marquises, our home,' she said.

My jaw dropped. Blushing, I groped for words. Calmly she pulled out a diary, took my phone number and asked me to visit on a day the following week, at 10am.

I drove back to my hotel in a daze. The Laurents were known to be elusive when it came to receiving private visitors. This was an ancient dream coming true.

I spent time and care choosing a present and gathering more information on their history. The family had been in Beaucaire for generations but it was Paul Laurent, Henri's father, who fell in love with the black bulls. An accomplished businessman, he ran a well-diversified agricultural enterprise, growing a variety of wine grapes and olives while breeding cattle and the renowned Arles Merino sheep. In spite of his high workload he still found time to live his dream of getting close to the black bulls. Due to passion and an unwavering sense of loyalty, he soon found favour with long-established ranchers in the Camargue by helping them round up bulls at dawn or during emergencies, day or night. Eventually he felt confident and proficient enough to establish his own *manade*. In 1944 he bought a few cows and bulls and settled them on his *mas*, a farm he owned near town. Soon his herd grew larger and he began to search for a property better suited to the semi-wild lifestyle of the animals. In the heart of the Camargue he found a slightly neglected stately property dating back to the early eighteenth century – Les Marquises. The estate had been given by Louis XIV to one of his victorious generals for battles won. The main house was surrounded by barns, cottages and 500 hectares of land. With patience and skill he renovated the buildings and then concentrated on creating a bull breed soon known for its intelligence and spirited, aggressive temperament.

Courses Camarguaises were run in a haphazard way in those days and he feared the tradition could be lost forever. To stop the rot, he began to modernise the competitions, improving the protection of the animals while in the ring. He could do so because he had acquired the right to manage several of the best-known arenas. Quickly he established a framework of rules for man and beast that led to a golden era lasting from the 1960s well into the 1980s. As an incentive for all *manadiers* to aim high, he and two friends introduced the *Biòu d'Or*, the golden trophy for the best bull judged by his performance throughout the entire year. Paul Laurent and his son Henri were soon unbeatable and, more often than not, envied as they alone collected the *Biòu d'Or* twelve times. Yet nobody can deny that their work for the Camargue and the protection of its nature and traditions soon proved invaluable.

Annie's family also had roots in the region. Up to the nineteenth century the Lescots had been wine growers near Lyon until the phylloxera aphid, an insect poisoning the roots of a vine, devastated the French wine industry. The Lescots migrated to the Camargue to rebuild their lives from scratch. Raising Merino sheep offered a new livelihood but, like the Laurents, they soon fell under the spell of the bull and Lescot became a name to be reckoned with.

On the big day, Annie Laurent rang early in the morning to give me directions on how to find them. She seemed surprised that I already knew how to reach the well-hidden empire; I had studied detailed large-scale maps.

Slowly I drove the main road to the seaside and the salt flats of Salin de Giraud. This felt like a pilgrimage. Halfway down I turned right onto a long white-gravelled dirt track which, after a few kilometres, changed into a narrow path flanked by trenches and dense, hardy bushes. A heron watched me passing by without budging. A beaver-like animal slowly crossed the track, lost in contemplation. Gaps either side of the path allowed glimpses of black bulls taking their morning nap. None of these animals felt disturbed or threatened. There was a powerful sense of peace.

I reached a tall iron gate. Its curved wings opened silently, giving access to an immaculate park. Sizeable farm buildings were dominated

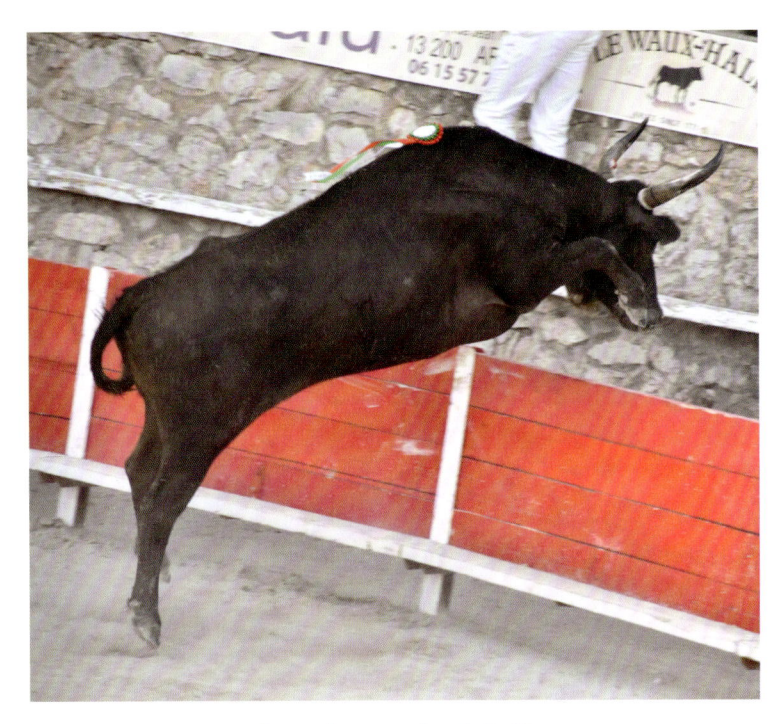

Barricades are no obstacle for Titan

by the main house, Les Marquises. One wall was adorned with the massive sculpture of a bull's head. Two dogs gave me a friendly greeting and soon Annie Laurent emerged, dressed in traditional garb complete with black fedora, to invite me in. She was formal yet warm-hearted.

The house turned out to be a living museum of the Camargue. Annie gave me a tour of the ground floor. Starting in a large but cosy kitchen decorated with a collection of polished horse bridles dangling from the ceiling, she led me to two vast rooms filled with regional antiques. One served as a salon and the other, a dining room with a gigantic table easily seating fifteen guests, had a fireplace the size of a London studio flat. Trophies occupied every surface and hundreds of photos told the story of both their families and famous visitors. Les Marquises had always attracted celebrities and the Laurents welcomed them with open arms. Other pictures showed their journeys across the world as ambassadors for the culture of the Camargue. The walls displayed paintings by known local artists with an astonishing stylistic variety. In spite of the multitude of items nothing looked cluttered. Not a speck of dust was to be seen. The housewife in me came out and I asked Annie: 'How do you keep it so clean in such a dust-prone environment?'

'I get up at five in the morning,' she said with a shy smile.

I thought they would have employed a cleaner for such a big house, but it was likely that she preferred dealing with delicate items herself.

Two small rooms deeply touched my heart. Next to the salon was a chapel. It looked a little like a grotto. *Santons*, the typically Provençal tiny figurines carved from wood – shepherds, peasants, sheep and other animals – stood in one corner. At the end, a small statue of the Virgin Mary dominated the scene. The chapel was bright and it offered simplicity, protection and serenity.

The other tiny room was dedicated to a trinity. A large oil portrait of Paul Laurent was flanked by two preserved bull heads, those of Goya and his father Loustic, complemented by Paul Laurent's saddle as well as paintings and memorabilia filling every space. All three of the trinity seemed to look down on me with calm interest. This was the heart of the house; this was the foundation of everything they lived for.

We sat down just in time for Henri to arrive. Looking at him, all muscles and not an ounce of fat visible, I couldn't believe that he was close to eighty. They were both extremely fit and out on horseback most days. The conversation over cups of coffee served in thin porcelain

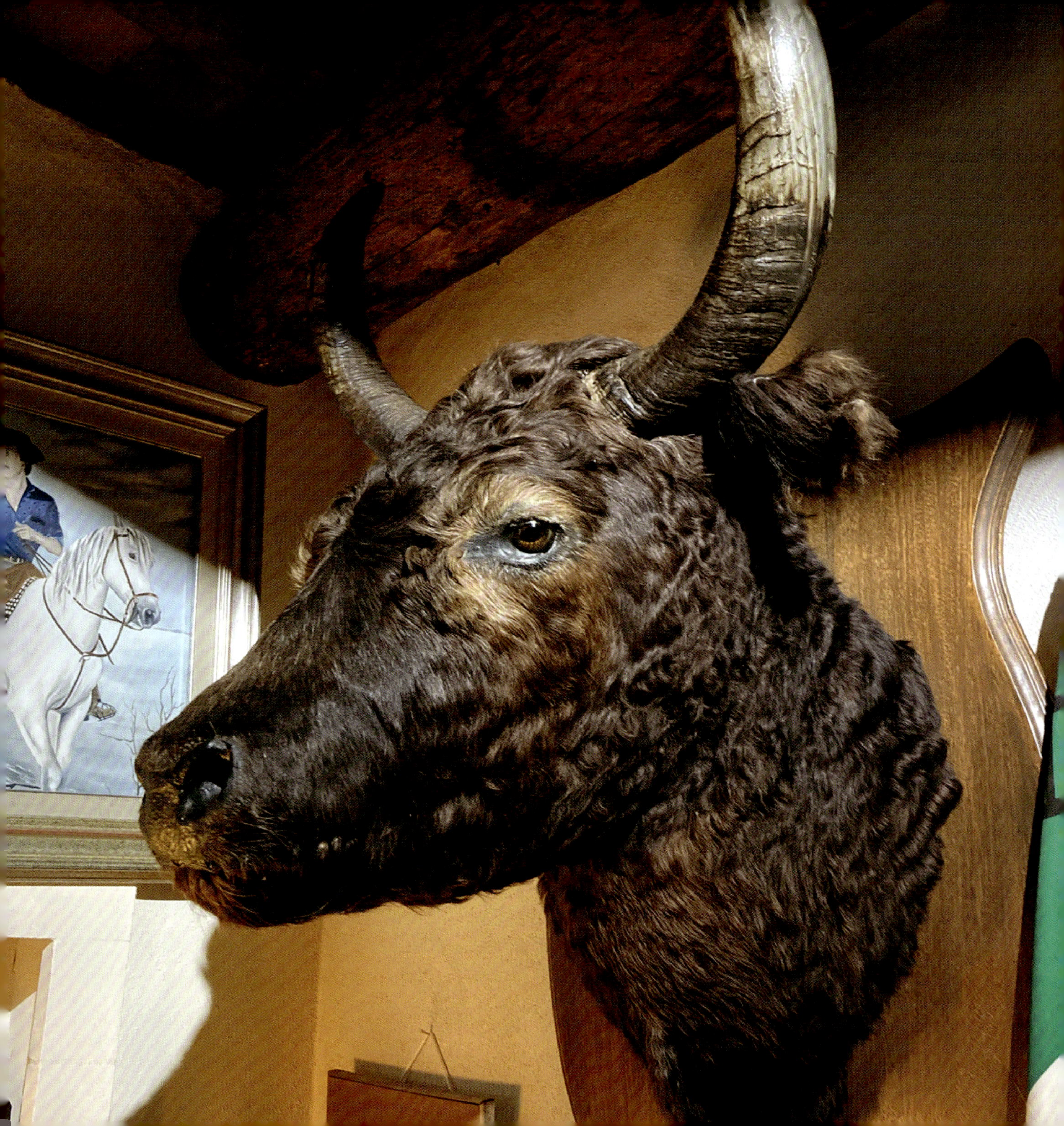

cups turned around the phenomenon of passion. They found it unusual for a foreigner to fall so whole-heartedly for their traditions. The atmosphere was still formal but the lively exchange about attitudes to growing older, life, the preservation of nature and curiosity about each other's history soon melted any remaining ice. Often the conversation turned to Paul Laurent who had passed away in 1989. Henri admitted that even now, decades after his death, not a single day passed without him thinking of his father, his warm-heartedness, his wisdom and his passion. Father and son had worked hand-in-glove and the same applied now: the family ran the *manade* as a closely knit team. Patrick's wife, Estelle, whose academic background couldn't be further from life in the wild, had quickly taken on a vital role herself, integrating into a family used to pulling together. Alongside dealing with the high workload at the ranch, she also acted as president of the regional commercial court. This is rare – only ten women have achieved this office among 134 presidents nationwide.

It worried me that they had named their only son, now ten years old, after his great-grandfather but Annie said nobody would force young Paul to live up to his illustrious ancestor. Yet, early signs indicated that he might.

An hour later we sat in a pick-up truck for a tour of the surrounding land. For the first time ever I had the privilege of seeing the precious semi-wild bulls and horses at close range. Both the Laurents, their son Patrick and their daughter-in-law spent their lives guarding and protecting this treasure with iron discipline and total humility towards nature's creation. Their territory, basking in the sun, seemed endless. Their home, their land and all the creatures in their care breathed a tranquillity and clarity I had rarely experienced before.

Passionately Henri explained what grew where and why. They

Opposite: Goya forever

had been among the first to grow organic rice and they practised crop rotation, allowing fields to recover between hay and rice harvests or being used as pasture. A sophisticated irrigation system was in place, fed by the Rhône. With pride he pointed out a new generation of young bulls, scattered over dozens of hectares and ready to tackle the bullring.

'How often do they run?' I asked.

'In the past they would appear every four weeks. That way they had time to recover and yet, it was regular enough for them to learn and gain experience. Goya was so fit that he could run every two weeks – we would have known if he didn't want to compete but he seemed to relish it. He was even waiting at the gates to be loaded up for each of his journeys to glory. These days the *Courses Camarguaises* are more popular than ever and there are far more bulls running than in the past, with each one performing less often.'

I was surprised when he mentioned that their mothers are nearly as important as the proud dad when it comes to characteristics: cows too carry a belligerent, combative gene and there are even competitions for "lady bulls".

Last we visited the bulls I had seen in Palavas; they were in a small group separate from other herds. Henri called them his "babies" and I wondered why.

'We had a great loss a few years ago. We had to start from scratch.'

Wiping a tear from the corner of his eye he mumbled that he couldn't talk about it because the memory was still too painful.

It was time to leave; they had work to do in the afternoon.

'How long are you staying?' Annie asked.

'At least four weeks.'

With a warm smile she said that I should come back. This went beyond my wildest dreams.

'I want to learn more,' I blurted out. 'Can you teach me?'

'We'll see,' Henri replied with a mysterious grin.

We parted with a far less formal traditional embrace and both waved until I was out of sight.

Emotionally overwhelmed by what I had seen and experienced, I stopped on the way back near the big lagoon, the Étang de Vaccarès. Flamingos grazed in the shallow water. I sat down on a rock. Looking out over the calm, glassy water surface it felt as if my life had taken a new, unexpected turn.

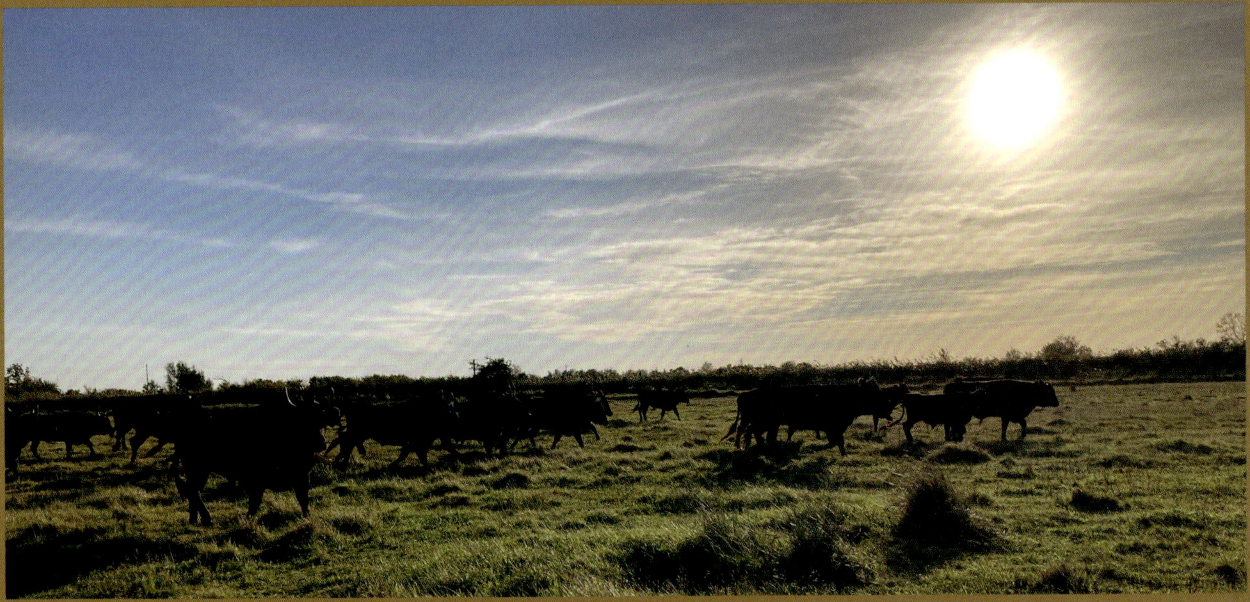

Chapter 3

Phoenix Rises From The Ashes

The family trees of illustrious bulls are of biblical length. Not to know that Goya's parents' names were Loustic and Blonde shows disqualifying ignorance. There was nothing "blonde" about Blonde – cows are just as belligerent and intelligent as their male counterparts, sometimes just as willing to defend the honour of their *manade* in the arena. Blonde had been above average and her mate Loustic had won the *Biòu d'Or* three times.

Goya's grandfather, Vovo, made his career in the 1950s before Paul Laurent introduced a more orderly system of competitions, leagues and prizes but Vovo's fame is, to this day, legendary. Very peaceful at home, he turned his every public appearance into a spectacular sequence of destruction. *Raseteurs* dreaded his speedy violence and barely dared approach him. During the fifteen minutes of each bull's time in the arena everybody can make bids, not in order to win anything but to raise the prize money for the *raseteurs*, thus encouraging them to make every effort to deprive the bull of his tassels and strings. In Vovo's case not even 320,000 francs, a fortune in those days, could tempt them to take him on. Often feeling under-occupied by his challengers, Vovo turned his attention to wrecking barricades and whatever else he could find in his way. In Lunel he demolished forty-eight supporting beams of the tribunes, seating thousands of spectators who narrowly escaped the impending collapse of the entire structure. Insiders argued for decades about whether he was a champion or just a destructive force out of control. The wider public had decided on the former, feeding Vovo's legend for decades to come.

To explore the Camargue in depth I needed a semi-permanent base. After several experiences of trial and error I found the perfect spot. The Domaine des Clos, ideally located in a rural area between Beaucaire and Arles, was a seventeenth century winery which had been converted into a hotel offering rooms as well as apartments to rent. The owners, Sandrine and David, had pursued successful business careers in Paris until three boisterous kids and the notoriously cramped conditions in the capital had them all longing for the open skies of their homeland. It was risky to buy a vast, dilapidated property and embark on a hospitality career they knew little about, but the risk paid off. With patience and a lot of hard, physical work, they restored the array of massive buildings and used the surrounding four hectares to create an Italianate park and olive groves. The moment I arrived I felt at home and the relationship between us quickly evolved into more than the usual guest-host relationship. They were intrigued by this new client obsessed with bulls, often coming home covered in

Two youngsters testing their strength

the dust and sand of the Camargue plains. They freely admitted to know little about the exotic culture right on their doorstep. Soon a lively exchange developed with me learning more about the colourful history of Provençe and Languedoc over opulent dinners accompanied by the song of a nightingale.

Visits to the Laurents, only a forty-minute drive away from the hotel, became more frequent and each time it felt like visiting a Holy Grail. There are other famous and older *manades* and every one of them has their dedicated community of fans. Yet I couldn't imagine anywhere else where a total stranger would be embraced with such a warm heart, where all animals and the surrounding nature were held in such high respect and loved beyond their owners' own lives.

Usually I arrived in the morning and we began, before having an extensive lunch, with a tour in a pick-up truck to check on the wellbeing of 300 bulls and cows scattered over 500 hectares, living in separate groups.

I was hungry to learn as much as I could and bombarded Henri with questions. How do you spot talent? Not every bull has the aptitude to enter the ring. How do you decide which bull is kept intact for breeding and when? The Laurents had won twelve *Biòu d'Or*, more than anybody else. What was the secret of their much envied success? Patiently, Henri explained it all.

Calmly steering the vehicle across the mix of wetland and prairie, through ditches, barely visible deep holes and thorny bushes, he said: 'It's passion, patience and observation.'

Stopping every now and then, he pointed out individual animals and their characteristics.

'You see, each one is different. You look into their eyes, you notice how alert and conscious they are of what goes on around them. Look at how they move, at the body frame. All of them are beautiful but some are stronger, more alert than others. These are wild animals, you can never tame them and you have no influence over breeding other than choosing a promising bull.'

I learned that calves are born in early spring and kept well hidden by their mothers before being introduced to the herd, approximately a week after their birth. The moment they become visible, observation begins. For one year they are free to roam. Their first contact with humans is unpleasant. The law requires vaccinations plus ugly ear clips and they have to be branded in order to identify them. The worst part for them is being captured because they don't know that it will be only for a few minutes. The branding itself is less painful than it looks as their skin is five millimetres thick. Approaching adolescence, the Laurents introduce them to small, local arenas. In a gentle, rather playful way they are confronted either with student *raseteurs* who are as inexperienced as the young bulls themselves or selected veterans who know how to test young talent without frightening them off. In their fourth year they may start competing in earnest.

That fourth year is decisive in many ways: a bull will be "christened". The name is always chosen in relation to his temperament or his ancestors and it carries all hope for a successful future. This is also the year when they have to decide to finally castrate or not. "Full" bulls, *taureaux entiers*, enjoy very high esteem and the best have the status of "stallion", *étalon*, which, in the rest of the world, is reserved for horses.

Henri pointed out a massive bull with an enormous chest and neck muscles that would have made Arnold Schwarzenegger look puny.

'Look, that's Cesar. He has been in various arenas and he is fantastic; everybody fears him. He could have a great career but he would hurt himself because he is so powerful. Vovo died relatively young, at the age of fourteen and it's like losing a family member. We will keep Cesar for breeding only. Let him enjoy himself!'

Prior to that decision there had been long deliberations between Henri and his son Patrick. Not allowing Cesar to run any more meant losing a sure winner but they agreed he might pass his talent on to future generations of potential stars. Goya, for example, would have made a brilliant stallion but the family wanted him to have a long career and a long life. Once castrated, bulls become calmer and more deliberate in their actions, more focussed on their task in the ring. Over three generations the Laurents had always acted using this slow, careful approach, putting the welfare of their animals before short-term success. It had always paid off.

I couldn't forget the tear I had seen in Henri's eye. I had read that something dreadful had happened in 2005, a catastrophe. They had lost their entire herd of 500 animals. As tactfully as possible I asked

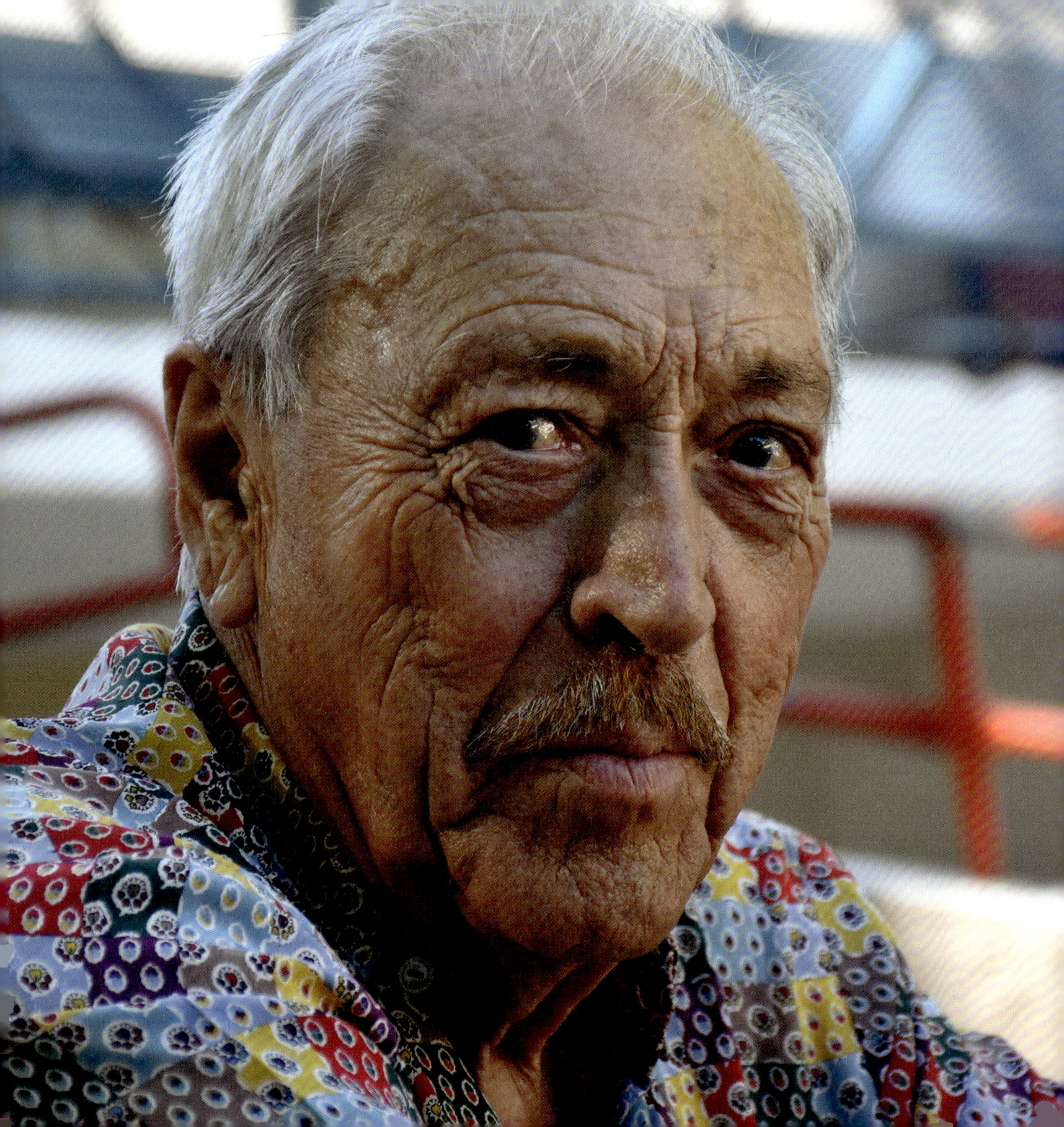

Henri what had happened. He stopped the truck and sighed.

'I still find it very difficult to talk about it,' he said.

His normally deep, powerful voice faded into a croak.

'I will tell you later,' he said.

When he did tell me, it was heartbreaking. In the early 2000s, an infectious disease hit the bovine population of the Camargue. In spite of meticulous precautionary measures, seven out of 500 animals at the Laurents were suspected of carrying the disease in 2005. Other ranches were affected as well. The Camargue bull is unique in the entire world. In spite of this and in spite of the tiny number of animals testing positive, without any further proof, the law at the time dictated that the entire herd had to be destroyed – sixty years of careful breeding extinguished like the flame of a candle. I cannot imagine what it felt like, watching these precious creatures, each one known by their name, each one representing family history, being loaded into trucks never to return. Their star bulls were the last to leave.

Slowly a deadly silence had descended on the Les Marquises, seat of the Manade Laurent. And yet, there was a glimmer of hope. If there was any future at all, it rested in the freezer of a laboratory. Some time before this, an instinct had led Henri and Patrick, who had experience with *in vitro* fertilisation for horses in the USA, to take sperm from two stallions, Lion and Teflon. Their family tree reached back over nearly 100 years and was in direct line back to Vovo and Loustic. This precious sperm was kept at minus seventy degrees Celsius and had to be regularly checked. Each check carried the danger of cells dying off.

When the death sentence following the outbreak hit the ranch, frantic negotiations began with the authorities. It was the beginning of a difficult and cruel process. The Laurents went on their knees, pleading to keep some of the best and disease-free cows for a period

Opposite: Henri Laurent on full alert in an arena

Voltaire wearing cocarde, tassels, strings and the colours of the Manade Laurent

of fifteen days. Permission was granted and in a hurry the sperm was transferred. Two weeks later embryos had formed. They were taken out of the doomed cows and transplanted into ordinary milk cows who would serve as surrogate mothers. These were sent to a different ranch belonging to the Laurents because the pasture at Les Marquises was still under quarantine. The Mas d'Assac, the second family property near Beaucaire, was also better suited to domesticated cattle.

An anxious wait began. For a long time, day after day, the family looked out over their deserted plains, hoping and praying that life would return. Even the horses looked lost.

For a while there was no income either. Nearly all ranches need tourism to maintain their passion for these bulls and keeping these animals often costs more than they ship in. Once the land was declared disease-free, the Laurents decided to buy a number of Camargue cows, thus building a basis for their new herd. The shows for tourists, marriage ceremonies and other events resumed. None of these visitors caught even a glimpse of the trauma the family lived through.

Carefully monitoring the cows fifty kilometres further north, the anxious wait continued. After nine and a half months the cows began to give birth. Over twenty healthy calves were safely delivered, enough to maintain the invaluable bloodline with a sufficiently broad gene pool. Once weaned off and able to feed themselves, they could travel home to their ancestral grounds. The arrival of these toddlers at Les Marquises meant the rebirth of a dynasty – now there would be a new start. Henri asked two rancher friends, whose animals also went back to the same bloodline, to sell him more bulls. As the Laurents had always gone out of their way to help others in times of need, he received quality animals to secure the future of their newly born ancient breed.

By using a complicated method never tried before with the wild bulls of the Camargue, they had banked a fortune on their revival and they had won. It would still take four long years to see if legendary success could be recreated. And, thankfully, the veterinary law has changed since: only individual creatures under strong suspicion of carrying a disease have to be removed.

There was one welcome interruption during the anxious wait. In 2008 Henri Laurent became *chevalier de la Légion d'honneur* in recognition of his lifelong service to the Camargue, in France and abroad. During an emotional speech he dedicated the honour to his father, Paul Laurent.

The Laurent bulls I had seen on my return to the Camargue in the arena of Palavas in 2013 were the result of a dangerous and painful experiment. Now fully grown and experienced, they had been defending the colours of their *manade* – white, green and red – for the first time in a premier league competition and they had done well. One of them was called Jupiter, a name carrying a huge amount of hope.

During each visit Annie and Henri taught me more about every aspect of their culture and history. The desire to be allowed to assist, to be in physical touch with anything that kept this paradise going, became painfully strong. Since childhood I had always spent all my spare time working on farms, at riding schools or animal rescue centres and I was used to dealing with all kinds of animals, from the tallest camel to the tiniest parrot. Confined or forced to stay separated from flora and fauna for longer periods of time is anathema to me and I get seriously depressed.

Here I was in the midst of a wonderland – if they would only allow me to do a little bit. Just sweeping the holy ground beneath the saintly hooves of their divine horses would have given me heavenly joy!

Apparently my prayers had been heard. The vast grounds were divided not only by natural barriers but also by fences and large gates. One day Henri asked me to open one of these gates for our vehicle to pass through. Finally there was something to do but it turned out to be tricky. Instead of simple levers there was a mechanism to operate. I looked at it and fumbled around without much success. Meanwhile two dozen young bulls had approached but did not come dangerously close. They just stood there, completely still. Twenty-four pairs of curious eyes stared at me, mesmerised by my vain attempts to open the gate. Pleadingly I turned around, seeking assistance, but Henri stayed behind his steering wheel, shrugging his shoulders as if to say 'If you can't even open a gate…'

Finally the penny dropped. Lifting little lids on steel tubes while simultaneously moving the levers did the trick. Relieved, I got back into the car.

'Catch me if you can'

'You've just passed the first test for an apprenticeship as a *gardian*,' he said, half joking. At least I hadn't completely stumbled at the first hurdle.

The locks are double and triple secured because bulls had learned how to open the gates themselves, in teamwork. And there is a reason why we always go on patrol by car. You can't approach on foot because they might fancy attacking. Approaching by horse usually means rounding up to be transported to an arena and every single bull will make this as difficult as possible. Most of them don't like leaving home, not even in the comfort of specially configured straw-lined trucks. The white pick-up Toyota, however, is not seen as any threat or disturbance to nibbling, ruminating or playing, and sometimes fighting with mates. It also allows getting close to individual animals to check on a limp, a bruise or any kind of unusual behaviour.

Whenever a Laurent bull took part in a *Course Camarguaise*,

I went to watch, even if it meant several hours of driving. For *manadiers* this is an opportunity to meet their colleagues and friends to exchange news or discuss problems.

Always surrounded by myriads of people, Henri still found time to teach me how to recognise the qualities of a good competitor. Slowly I learned to judge for myself how well a bull positioned himself, how quick he was at anticipating the movements of his two-legged challengers or how willing he was to take on a *raseteur* and, above all, how good he was at finishing his actions by chasing his opponent right up to the barricades.

Each animal going into the ring requires careful management. I was surprised to learn that bulls can get depression.

'At times,' Henri explained, 'the *raseteurs* are too aggressive in their eagerness to score points. They descend like a white swarm on a bull and if he can't get hold of any of them, he feels demoralised.'

I love the fact that occasionally they withdraw a beast from competitions to give it time to recover mentally, even if this decision causes conflict with the organisers of events. A whole range of factors put the bulls at a disadvantage. The *raseteurs* have become more and more athletic and, in the interest of their safety, the walls surrounding the ring and the aisle are equipped with metal grips, allowing for an easier escape. Remembering how much visible joy Goya had shown when chasing people successfully, I understand a bull's frustration perfectly well when, time and gain, he runs into empty space.

By now the new generation of bulls belonging to Henri and Patrick had more experience and seven of them were doing very well. Yet, each time one of their "babies" entered the ring, Henri's eyes narrowed, his breathing accelerated and he couldn't sit still. Every *manadier* fears his animals being accidentally injured or hurting themselves due to their own powerful actions, but for the Laurents this was even more stressful. So much had been invested, so much anguish and grief had been suffered to see a revival. I could hear a discreet sigh of relief whenever the action-filled fifteen minutes were up and his bulls left the arena safely, more often than not under applause and blasting trumpets.

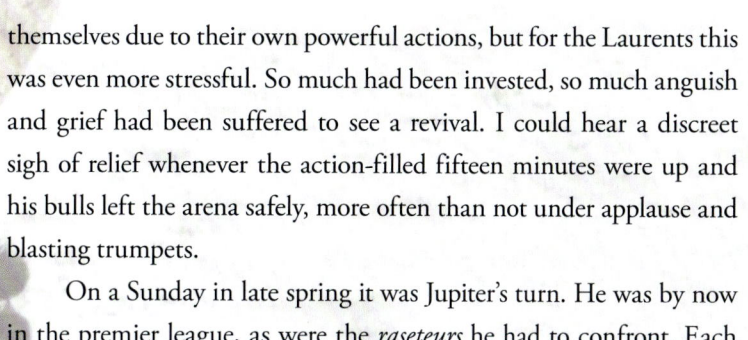

On a Sunday in late spring it was Jupiter's turn. He was by now in the premier league, as were the *raseteurs* he had to confront. Each competition counted towards the *Biòu d'Or* and the *Trophée des As*, the coveted annual prize for top *raseteurs*.

It all began slowly. Ten men watched Jupiter and Jupiter eyed them. When the first *raseteur* made a run for him, all the others followed suit, in a sequence. As if he knew what was expected, Jupiter didn't refuse a single attack which he could have done simply by standing still.

'He's so generous,' I heard Henri whispering.

After seven minutes he had lost his red ribbon and the two tassels but he viciously defended his *ficelles*, the strings around his horns. Any *raseteur* running past, inviting the bull to follow, thus giving an opportunity to touch the horns, failed. Jupiter required four or five steps to reach full speed and some of the young men underestimated his power. Like a heat-seeking missile, he stayed glued to his potential victim no matter which way they went, following them straight to the barricades and over, even trying to jump up the wall they hung on to for dear life. When the trumpet sounded, he calmly trotted off. Standing ovations followed until he had disappeared from sight. Jupiter was definitely a fast-rising star.

It became harder and harder for me to return to London. The journey back was always a chore. The Eurotunnel train seemed dirtier than on the way out. Clouds seemed to hang lower. Yes, I had a beautiful flat and friends but life back home had become too mundane. There were no bulls in London. How can one live without bulls? The consolation was in my car. It groaned under the load of books, olive oil, herbs and, for special occasions, bull's meat. I used the drab winter months to study, wolfing down books as if my life depended on it. In a way it did. Henri had already spent a lot of time teaching me and I didn't want to disappoint him. The study of history, customs and literature of the Camargue became even more fascinating by having a mentor who was a living example of it all.

While reading, I sometimes look up into grey skies, but I've never again seen a cloud shaped like a bull. Perhaps they don't appear

Lavender field in the garden of Van Gogh's hospital in Saint-Rémy-de-Provence

because they are no longer needed; the bulls are close to my heart even when over 1000 kilometres away. So are the memories of endless poppy fields, of Van Gogh's sunflowers spread over miles and of endless rows of lavender, buzzing with bees and butterflies. Nothing can lift the soul more than sitting in a sun-flooded lavender field. Stroking a bush upwards invites it to release clouds of scent, turning my head dizzy with happiness.

Then there are Annie's presents to bridge the winter drought. She has never allowed me to leave empty-handed. One day she shared half of her jar of *fleur de sel* with me. This coarse salt with its rich, nearly oily taste is hand-harvested. It's a skill to carefully lift it off the surface of the sun-dried salt flats near Salin de Giraud. Annie has her private source for this delicacy which makes it even more precious to me. Next to my laptop sits a large shell she had found in the fields. This land has been cultivated for ages and I believe that the shell, once left by the receding sea, must have been many thousand years old. I love these presents of nature even more than all the regional food items she often prepares for me to take home.

Over the years a collection has built up and one of its rarest items is Magali's horn. All bulls have to go through regular vaccinations or other veterinary treatment. For the safety of everybody they are channelled into a short but narrow wooden tunnel which leaves little room to start a fight. Treatment is given through gaps. Every now and then an unruly animal will try to escape while entering the unfamiliar tunnel. And a horn can be bent or lost, which is what had happened to a young Magali. No further harm was done; she went on to become the proud mother of very successful fighters and still enjoys rude health. Looking at her horn dangling from a desk lamp always triggers an intense longing to be back with Annie and Henri, back with them under open skies.

Memories like these help to survive the cold season, but every year as early as February I grow increasingly restless. It is tempting to drive down and experience frosty, clear Camargue air under a pale sun, but all of Provençe is closed down – there isn't much to do for me and usually I have to wait until April to head south and take up residence in the hotel apartment that has become a second home.

Normally the Camargue bulls feed on what the soil offers them. During harsh winters or cold springs they will get additional quality hay because they can no longer roam over hundreds of miles as they may have done before humans appeared. Bulls who do well in the arena are called *cocardiers*. The seven best of the Laurent herd have their own fifty hectares, near the main house, to play and to snooze.

I was absolutely delighted when Annie and Henri invited me to feed them. Like high-performance athletes, they received diet supplements in the form of dark, rich oats. We walked into an area partly sheltered by trees and bushes where seven stone bowls had been lowered into the ground. Water troughs were nearby. Instantly I called it the "*Restaurant des cocardiers*". The only thing missing was napkins.

'Where are they? How is it that we can just walk in?'

Both told me not to worry because, at this time of the day, the gang enjoyed their siesta hidden away under trees in the shade. We began to fill the bowls, each portion carefully measured. I was just about to fill one at the far end. Annie and Henri were at the other end of the field. Suddenly I noticed that they had stopped moving. They stood still as if frozen in time, looking in my direction and beyond. Slowly I turned my head. Behind me, not more than ten metres away, stood Jupiter, on full alert. Noiselessly he had appeared out of nowhere and now he was pondering what to do. He recognised his parents but I was a stranger. If you are approached by a charging bull,

Aragon visits his audience – no harm done to either

the only slim chance to avoid injury or worse is to throw yourself flat on the ground. In the given situation this was impossible; he was too close. Quickly I averted my eyes, signalling peace. He didn't lower his head – a good sign. Slowly, very slowly, I carried on pouring oats into his bowl, hoping that his favourite food would appease him. It did. I started inching away from the full bowl, tiny step by step, until I had reached a safe distance. He gave me one last, not unfriendly look and began to inspect his dinner.

An approving smile from Annie and Henri indicated that I had done the right thing. Even a while afterwards I couldn't recall any fear. The memory remains one of utter beauty and privilege to be so near such a magnificent animal.

In a week's time Jupiter would go into another big competition. I wondered if he knew how much hope and responsibility rested on his

The sunflowers Van Gogh loved so much

mighty goblet-shaped horns. His biggest co-competitor came from the Manade Paulin, carrying the seductive name Cupidon. The Camargue community was somewhat divided between Jupiter and Cupidon. It was still a few months to go before a jury of twenty-four would decide on this year's winner of the *Biòu d'Or*. The race was on. Each one of Jupiter's performances had been flawless. He dominated the ring, always finding the most favourable position to keep the *raseteur*s in check and going after them the moment anyone made the slightest move for his tassels. Some hoped that inviting him for a futile chase into empty space would tire him out and create an opportunity to get near enough to his head – no chance.

How the jury decides on the winner of the gold trophy has always been shrouded in mystery. They seem to be like the Vatican curia and the result has often been hotly contested.

The season neared its end, the election was due and the Camargue waited anxiously for white smoke to emerge. A few days before the decision fell, Annie rang to let me know that a twenty-fifth vote had been given to the public – we could vote online. With only a few days left, I mobilised everybody I knew to support Jupiter.

I was back in London when the result was announced. The curia had a split vote of twelve to twelve but the public had tipped the balance in favour of Jupiter – he had done it! Jupiter carried home the thirteenth *Biòu d'Or* for the Manade Laurent! They dedicated it to young Paul and online I saw him receiving the trophy in the arena. He clutched it in his arms, beaming. He was still only fourteen years old but had already developed into an excellent rider, familiar with any and every task a *gardian* has to master. Annie invited me for the grand evening of celebration a few weeks later but I couldn't leave London. To know that the Phoenix had truly risen from the ashes made up for it.

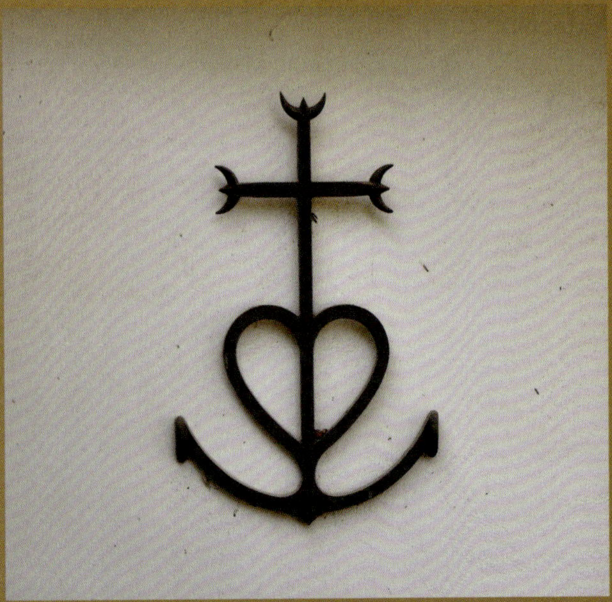
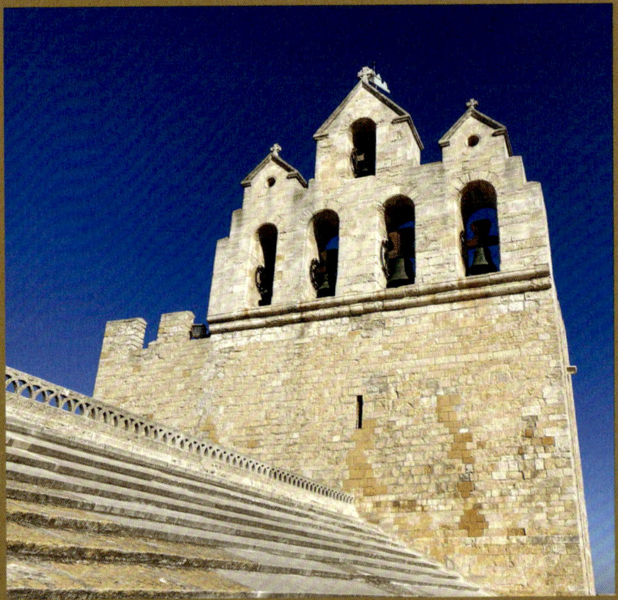

Chapter 4

The Mad Marquis

It was early April and I was greeted by torrential rain on arrival at my friends' hotel. Annie rang and invited me to help with feeding the herd. After a rough winter the animals needed a little bit of culinary assistance as their pastures had not yet fully grown back. Most ranches rely on a wide circle of friends and volunteers to help out during peaks of work. Any invitation to help out at a *manade* is an honour and I couldn't wait to be with them. On the day, I was up at six in the morning, eager to get there on time and fully equipped with the foul-weather gear she had advised me to bring.

A long flatbed trailer, loaded with bales of home-grown quality hay and pulled by a tractor with gigantic wheels, was ready to conquer miles of prairie that had turned into a vast swamp. A *gardian* sat in a heated cabin behind the wheel while Annie and I clambered on to the trailer in freezing wind and rain.

'Watch out for Marlou! He's dangerous,' she said.

'How will I know which one is Marlou?'

'Oh, you'll know when he appears,' she smiled.

Reaching the first herd, we started dividing up hay parcels and threw them down, making sure they hit dry patches either side of the track. I soon tuned into the calm rhythm set by Annie. Bale strings had to be carefully stowed away and not left behind as they could entangle birds and other creatures. The bulls slowly followed us and there had to be space between the parcels so that each had a portion without having to fight over it. Watching out for unruly beasts, I swept back my hood to have an unobstructed view. Rain and hail driven by sharp gusts needled our faces and I felt water running down my neck and back.

Labouring to get from one herd to the next, the enormous tractor wheels kept grinding on, sometimes sinking half into the uneven soil and its often invisible holes. Glorious mud splattered us from head to toe. The trailer bed nearly touched the ground.

I was just about to cut open a particular bale when Annie stopped me.

'Don't – it's our cover.'

As soon as she had said it, a monstrous black ball with horns hurled itself onto the trailer. Two hundred and fifty kilos of bull hurtled towards us and we had only seconds to take cover. Marlou, nearly five years old at the time, was the angriest teenager bull I'd ever seen or heard of. Frustrated for not getting hold of us, he kept throwing his entire weight against the bales, his sharply pointed horns piercing the hay like daggers. Everything shook and swayed and we nearly lost one of the bales protecting us.

'So much for gratitude', I thought. Finally he relented and we could carry on.

Hours later, trundling back to the main house, I stretched out on the loading surface streaming with water. It didn't matter as I was soaked to the skin anyway, tired but happy. Annie, already in her early seventies, still looked fresh as a daisy. We tied the strings into neat little bundles. There were few words but I felt a sense of common accomplishment.

'You're used to farm work,' she finally stated, before adding: 'Marlou could go far, terrorising the arenas.'

He certainly would. After all, he had famous and noble ancestors. Having been inches away from his aristocratic headgear I began to wonder what the real fuss over bloodlines was. After all, these were beautiful but truly wild beasts that had been in the Rhône delta since the dawn of time. Who had started obsessing over their family trees and why?

Henri had often mentioned the name 'Baroncelli', followed by 'to whom we owe so much'. The man in question was an eccentric aristocrat who had breathed new life into a rather patchy regional culture. The Marquis Folco di Baroncelli, born in 1869, came from a Florentine family that had left Italy in 1365. They settled in Avignon and came to bankroll a line of French popes who stayed in France in opposition to the politics of the Vatican in Rome. The city of Avignon and surrounding territories were then part of the Papal States. Eventually unable to pay their debts to the Baroncellis, the French popes gave them a fiefdom together with the title of a Marquis near Carpentras and the Palais du Roure in Avignon, a grand semi-gothic pile. Nowadays it serves as a centre for all aspects of Provençal studies.

Young Folco spent all his holidays with his grandmother who owned a *mas*, a farmhouse in a small town of the western Camargue. Unusual for a member of the upper class, he grew up speaking not only French but Provençal as well, said to be only used by peasants and simple folk. From early on he was fascinated by local bull games, *gardians* and their horses. One day he apparently let a nosy cow into the kitchen and his grandmother was not pleased at all when the *gardians* had to widen a window aperture to get the beast back into the yard. Bulls aside, he studied Greek, German and Latin literature and began writing poetry in Provençal.

France in the mid-nineteenth century was embroiled in a massive culture war. Republican Paris wanted to centralise power by eliminating any sign of provincial autonomy. That meant suppressing regional languages, local customs and administrative structures.

Nowhere was the resistance greater than in the south of France. The Midi had been independent from France for centuries; it had always been influenced by culture, trade and people coming from Italy, Greece and Catalan Spain. Often you hear locals calling their region Occitanie. Normally opposed to each other, catholic Provence and protestant Languedoc joined forces to defend their *Occitan* identity. It is often said that while the Languedoc works, Provence sings. For a greater cause, tools were downed and the singing stopped. Pitchforks became weapons against military oppression. Even the bulls were turned into resistance fighters – and martyrs: at one of the now illegal bull games a regiment was sent in to shoot them. It caused a violent uproar, combined with calls to reinstate the monarchy.

In this boiling cauldron approaching civil war, a group of intellectuals called the *Félibrige* and led by Frédéric Mistral (1830–1914) saved the peace and achieved recognition for the endangered culture and its customs. Some of these well-educated idealists had to learn Provençal themselves before they could start defending it. The movement gathered momentum; Parisian literary circles were

The Baroncelli Museum in Saintes-Maries-de-la-Mer

fascinated by the poetry originating in what was generally considered one of the most unattractive backwaters of France.

In 1904 Frédéric Mistral was awarded the Nobel Prize for Literature – the only author to receive this award for a body of work published in a regional language. Tension between Paris and the Camargue had eased and local folk were once again allowed to live according to their festive traditions.

Folco di Baroncelli joined this group in the 1890s as a writer and editor of *l'Aïoli,* a magazine in Provençal published three times a month. Most of his fellow writers had no connection whatsoever to the ordinary people whose lifestyle they so ardently defended. Baroncelli, however, had a deep love for them and the soil they lived on.

The urge to own a *manade* became irresistible and in 1895 he rented a ranch near Saintes-Maries-de-la-Mer, a small fishing village by the sea. The Camargue in those days was truly wild, considered to be disease-infested and inhabited by primitives. Monks, owning the rich abbeys of the region, had begun to tame the rivers in the Middle Ages. They built a system of channels and dams to prevent flooding but still, the Camargue refused to be completely tamed by human effort.

Even today this landscape with its often abrupt and sometimes dangerous, inclement weather is a classic case of love-it-or-hate-it. Some people see it as a barren, monotonous expanse without any attraction to a beauty-seeking eye.

Folco's wife couldn't tolerate the swampy climate and moved back to Avignon, together with their three children. It didn't wreck the marriage and, more importantly, left him free to realise an absolutely mad idea: having studied Greek and Mesopotamian bull cults, he wanted to recreate the original black bull as he had seen it in ancient illustrations. The Camargue bull is said to have this heritage but a lot of the animals the Marquis saw did not comply with the ideal mythical figure.

Over many centuries people had tried to coax the beasts into serving a useful purpose. They attempted to use the cows for milk but their udders are tiny, just big enough to feed their own offspring. Pulling a cart or a plough was out of question for any self-respecting bull and they simply refused. A modest profit was gained through meat production but the animals were really too small, lean and muscular to give a viable yield. It was the driving of the animals to an abattoir which gave birth to the games. In the early Middle Ages they were subject to taunting by young men trying to touch the head or force them to the ground. Soon they discovered that these intelligent animals could be used for an exciting kind of entertainment and the first *Courses Camarguaises* took place in many farmyards across the region. This was an age where children had to grow into adults quickly in order to join the workforce. Specific entertainment for adolescents barely existed – the lucrative youth industry with its fashion, discos and electronic games was many centuries away. Playing with bulls became a popular pastime to relieve rural boredom.

In the later nineteenth century Spanish bullfight, the ritual killing of a bull in an arena, conquered parts of the south of France. Some breeders tried to cross the Iberian bull, an animal nearly double the size of the native variety, with the black Camargue bull. I had seen a few of these from afar. Their relatively short horns pointed forward and they looked rather placid. To me they were no comparison to the agile, alert black Camargue bull with its horns reaching for the skies.

It wasn't a success but any kind of game involving the animals began to gain them recognition and admiration. Slowly, rules evolved to protect them from abuse for the French version of games.

Folco di Baroncelli's highly un-scientific approach to prevent the disappearance of the noble animal of antiquity was simple. Among the recent, widely mixed hodgepodge of cows and bulls populating the Camargue, he found and bought those that were pitch black, had an athletic build and carried horns pointing upwards, preferably lyre- or goblet-shaped. He avoided any not corresponding to his ideal.

Over time, the family fortune had melted considerably; they had to sell the Palais de Roure but somehow he managed to acquire 326 animals. Further narrowing down his strict selection, he decided to keep the best 190. An accomplished horseman and familiar with the work of the *gardians*, he kept a close eye on their development. In the evenings he still wrote poems but his close cooperation with

Frédéric Mistral faded away; he was simply too busy recreating the mythical bull, the perfect bull. Realising that Baroncelli's obsession also contributed to a revival of Provençal culture, Mistral let him go without reproach.

Finally years of sacrifice and hard slog paid off. In 1901 a bull Baroncelli named Prouvènço entered the ring. By now people paid to see a French bullfight. Aggressive, bright and beautiful, Prouvènço proved to be a crowd puller. Fans came from far away to see this miracle animal in the arena and the *Course Camarguaise* gained fame, finally giving the black bulls their true *raison d'etre* and securing their future. Prouvènço had fulfilled Folco's dream of an ancient ideal.

Baroncelli's own life came to a miserable end. Spending every penny on buying bulls and maintaining his herd and pastures, he couldn't pay the rent for his farm. Eventually he was given a smaller property nearer the town but his health deteriorated, just as the Second World War broke out. In 1942 "Free France" wasn't free at all. The German army entered the Midi and his property was requisitioned by the occupiers with little regard for the value of black bulls. Some ranchers tried to hide their most precious animals to prevent them from ending up as rations for hungry troops. Baroncelli's farm was destroyed by soldiers on retreat, leaving only smouldering ruins behind.

His bad luck continued. Trying to save a horse, Baroncelli had an accident from which he would not recover. Virtually penniless, he died in an Avignon hospital in 1943.

All Laurent bulls, and those of a few other famous ranchers, are descendants of the prolific Prouvènço and Baroncelli's perfect herd. Now I understood the importance of this heritage and the obsession with family trees.

I went to Saintes-Maries-de-la-Mer to find traces of the Marquis.

The original fishing village, dating back to the days of Jesus, had grown into a sizeable tourist hotspot but thankfully the architecture with its low-slung, whitewashed buildings surrounding the massive fortified church had been preserved. There were a lot of newly built second homes but they all had to comply with strict regulations.

Originally Baroncelli had been buried in Avignon but his wish had been to rest on the site of his former *manade*, and four years after his death permission was granted to transfer him. The tomb can be found just outside town, looking towards the church of Notre Dame de la Mer. On top of a simple, circular concrete structure rests a stone catafalque containing his ashes. At the time of his funeral, his bulls are said to have followed the cortège with tears in their eyes. In a land so rich with legends and so reliant on mystery I decided to believe it. Seeing the tomb was disappointing: the site is squeezed between a busy road and a less-than-picturesque campsite. It was covered in weeds and trash. This came as a surprise because in general the Camargue was spotlessly clean with barely a trace of litter. Later I learned that the tomb is regularly cleaned up.

On to the Baroncelli Museum, a slender but stately building in the centre of the town. It was closed, had been for years. Had the Camargue forgotten her most dedicated and faithful son, the one who had given his life for them?

Far from it. The Marquis's legacy is very much alive and clearly noticeable. Whenever there is a major competition, there is a prelude with *gardians* displaying their skills. They are dressed in tight-fitting trousers made of moleskin, colourful shirts and scarves, waistcoats and wide-brimmed fedoras. This costume was developed by Baroncelli. The black velvet jacket completing the glamorous yet practical outfit was inspired by a close friend, the Russian artist Ivan Pranishnikoff.

Folco di Baroncelli's tomb in Saintes-Maries-de-la-Mer

In the old days a *gardian* had been considered a lowly farm worker. Usually poor, they wore shapeless, tattered garb and, more often than not, wooden clogs. *Gardians* of the past mostly worked on foot; leather boots wouldn't have lasted long when trudging through salty mud. Over time more of their work was done on horseback and Baroncelli's designer uniform gave them a new respected status. Today they wear the same costume, minus the velvet jacket, when working on the ranches because it's functional, comfortable and looks incredibly flattering. The Marquis had been extremely fashion-conscious and his original design had a few fancy additions which were soon discarded; the *gardians* found them too "prissy".

In a similar way he "fashioned up" the costume worn by the *Arlésiennes*, the women of Arles and the Camargue. To further reinforce the sense of regional identity, he founded the *Nacioun Gardiano*, a federation dedicated to the tribe of *gardians*. Nowadays he would be considered a master of public relations, capable of creating a "brand".

Knowing how powerful, how uniting symbols and rites can be, Baroncelli went further. In 1926 he asked the painter-illustrator Hermann-Paul to create the Camargue cross, *le croix de Camargue*. The final design consisted of three elements welded together in harmony: the trident, used by *gardians* to herd bulls, forms the cross to represent faith. The heart in the middle symbolises charity and the anchor below, a reference to the fishermen of the Camargue, eternalises hope. The cross quickly became popular. It can be seen everywhere – on pillars, on walls and at entrances to houses, often together with a depiction of a bull and a horse.

The revival of the Provençal language had been a success. The Laurents spoke it fluently. Out of curiosity I asked if they spoke Provençal when among themselves and I was surprised when Annie admitted, with a slightly sheepish smile, that they stuck to French. Perhaps she felt unfaithful but their preference may have to do with speed – somehow I have the impression that Provençal lends itself to a more oratorical style, while French can be rattled out at machine-gun speed.

To support "my" *manade*, I went to see a major competition in Saintes-Maries. The white arena, built close to the beach, offers no shade but was fully packed with tourists and locals who eagerly awaited the appearance of Marlou. By now the unruly four-legged Laurent teenager had turned into an adult. The atmosphere was festive and the tourists especially loved the splendid introductory displays of horsemanship, the music and the performance of the Amazons – ladies riding side-saddle.

A German couple sitting next to me had several cameras rolling. Their mood darkened when the first bull appeared. All *cocardiers*

– bulls experienced in the ring – wear the colours of their *manade* on their back in the form of badges with ribbons floating in the air. The woman next to me seemed shocked and appalled.

'How cruel to stick needles into the back of the poor animal!'

I pacified her by explaining that the badges are glued on, adding that the glue was water soluble.

'Aha.'

Marlou ran in pole position which always belongs to the fourth bull. Storming on to the sand, he was greeted by shouts and whistles of expectation. He didn't wait for the trumpet to sound the start of his fifteen minutes but jumped straight over the barricades in search of anything that moved. Cat-like speedy movements kept the *raseteurs* at bay; hardly anybody dared approach him. When someone did, they soon had to run for their lives before they could even attempt to touch his head, let alone pick off one of his tiny accolades. This bull had his eyes everywhere, with an extraordinary degree of anticipation. They tried and kept failing. Frustrated that he couldn't get hold of a victim, Marlou began to dismantle the barricades. Planks flew high up into the sky. The audience screamed with delight – except for the animal-loving woman.

'He's bleeding!' she complained.

'Where?' I asked.

'On his horns!'

I pointed out that the planks of the barricade are thickly coated with red paint which not only rubs off on a bull's horns but also stains the originally pure white trousers of the *raseteurs*. Finally she was at ease, only wondering if the red colour had the purpose of making the animals more aggressive. I shared a recently acquired bit of knowledge with her: bulls are partially colour-blind and do not see red. Red excites the onlooker, not the animals.

By now Marlou was chasing around an empty oval. When his time was up, he left under thundering applause and the tunes of *Carmen*, not without giving one last angry kick to the gate closing behind him.

The competition was over and Marlou had won the prime trophy. I went around the arena to the loading area to meet a happy Henri Laurent.

'He is impossible!' he said.

'I adore him!' I replied.

'Me too,' said Henri.

Still marvelling at Marlou's performance, we were suddenly distracted by Henri's truck we stood next to. The solid vehicle swayed from side to side and there was an almighty ruckus going on inside. Bulges and dents appeared on the pristine green bodywork of the vehicle, caused by Marlou butting the walls. Patrick and Nicolas, their chief *gardian*, had managed to get him inside but now they had problems securing him to the overhead rails, a fiddly job that has to be done lying on planks on the open roof of the truck. The rebellious spirit of the Camargue was truly alive and it took half an hour, a lot of swearing and quite a few bruised arms to get the star ready for travelling home.

The late afternoon sun cast a warm glow over the ancient town and I strolled over to the church that dominated the skyline. Approaching the fortified building dating back to the ninth century, I was accosted by dozens of Gypsies offering fortune-telling and "sacred" trinkets. Quickly I fled into the church. It was peaceful and quiet, so I lit a few candles for people and animals close to my heart. Over many centuries this fortified church had offered shelter whenever the town was under attack from Saracens, Vikings and marauders coming from the sea.

The presence of Roma Gypsies has tradition and is linked to one

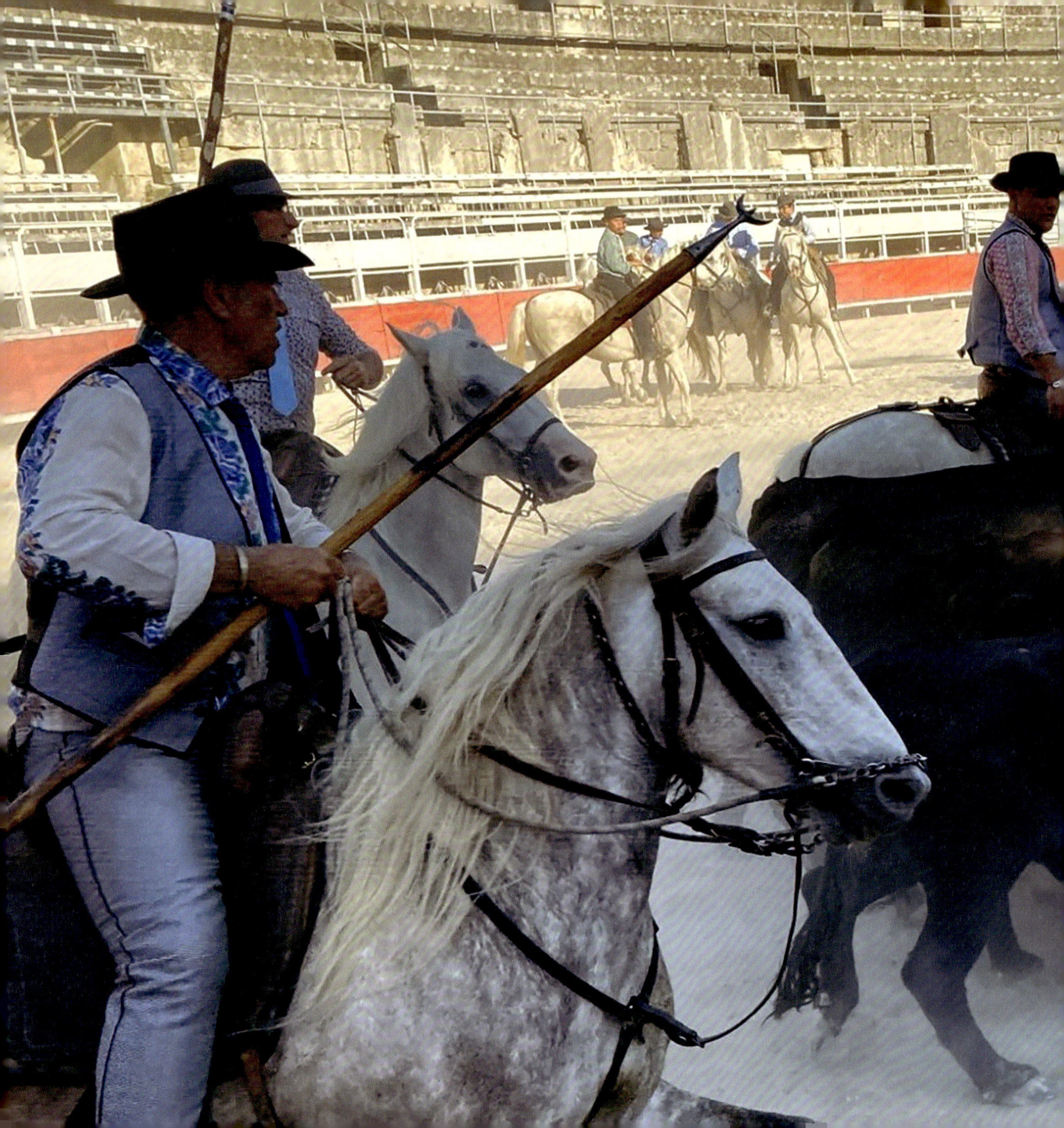

Gardians wearing the costume designed by Baroncelli

of the most powerful legends of the Camargue. Les Saintes Maries – Marie Magdalene, Marie Jacobé and Marie Salomé – belonged to a group of women who are believed to be the first witnesses to the empty tomb at the resurrection of Jesus. Driven out by the Romans, they drifted across the Mediterranean in a small boat without sails or oars. They arrived safely on the shores of this small fishing village. With them was the dark-skinned Sara who is said to have possibly been the servant of two of the Maries. Monks discovered relics of the Saints in the Middle Ages although sceptics point out that monks have a prolific talent for finding relics wherever and whenever there is a need for them.

The crypt holds a statue of Sainte Sara although she has never been officially canonised. Yet she is the most revered figure of the four: from the fifteenth century onwards the Roma began to believe that she was one of theirs, a Gypsy. Pilgrimages for the Maries had always existed but now the Roma began an annual ritual honouring "their Sainte". Originally this happened on a rather small scale.

Some Roma have been living near Saintes-Maries-de-la-Mer for centuries and they attracted the attention of Baroncelli. The romantic Marquis had a soft heart for minorities and he firmly believed that Sara was of noble descent, that she hailed from the mythical island of Atlantis and that she was the legitimate ancestor of all Roma in the south of France. He may have been poor but his voice was influential. Together with other members of the *Félibrige* he promoted the annual pilgrimage to become an official event. Under a barrage of letters and applications, the authorities and the Archbishop of Aix-en-Provençe gave permission in 1935 for the event to take place regularly – another successful legacy of the Marquis mad with passion for his chosen homeland. Ever since, the little town has been bursting at the seams each May, when colourful ceremonies attract tens of thousands of worshippers, tourists and an international set of pickpockets alike.

The small crypt radiates safety and hope. When I went to see it the first time, its walls and ceiling had been blackened by decades of candle smoke. Devotional pictures and cards with desperate pleas for divine help covered every inch. They were more numerous than the testimonies to prayers that had been favourably answered. Quite a few of these mementos were over 150 years old. The tiny statue of Sara stood in a corner, watching over it all.

As I left, a throng of Roma women surrounded me. Pleas to leave me alone fell on deaf ears. They only let go when I took to shouting unprintable expletives which were promptly answered by a shrieking cursing of the remaining days of my life.

During one of these remaining days I received another invitation from Annie and Henri. The church was built on the foundations of a Roman place of worship. Due to age and its exposure to the salty sea air the building requires constant renovation. A major milestone was achieved with the refurbishment of the crypt dedicated to Sainte Sara. The mayor had invited the Who's Who of the Camargue to celebrate the achievement. It was such a privilege that the Laurents allowed me to accompany them.

The long Provençal mass and the speeches afterwards bore testimony to the importance of religion in Camargue society. Strong voices sang with an intensity coming from the heart. I could feel that the peoples' interpretation of religion is not based on the teachings of a dogma; it rather celebrates immense gratitude and dedication to nature, rooted in the firm belief that all creatures are of equal value. I thought that's how it should be. How could it not be?

The official part over, we went down into the crypt. It was

freshly painted in white, looking more spacious than in the past. A lot of devotional messages had been removed and I don't know if I regretted the removal of hundreds of cluttered historic testimonials or favoured the cleaner, more serene atmosphere that now prevailed. Each one of us, lost in thought, lit candles, their flickering flames carrying hope for the future.

Saintes-Maries-de-la-Mer has only a population of less than 3000 inhabitants, but this can swell to several hundred thousand during holidays and the pilgrimage. It is called the capital of the Camargue and numerous shops lining the narrow streets reflect this reputation. Apart from a myriad of restaurants and tourist shops there are a lot of outlets catering for *manadiers* and *gardians*, selling everything from saddles, bridles and boots to traditional outfits and ordinary, good-quality household necessities. This town definitely has a life and an identity independent from the mass tourism it tolerates with good humour. I couldn't resist buying a pair of traditional *gardian* trousers. They fitted perfectly well but I decided not wear them while in the Camargue, thinking that tourists going native can look quite ridiculous.

Shopping done, I sat down on the promenade to look out over a peaceful sea. By now I was no longer an outsider but I was clearly not one of them either and this was perfectly logical. Unless you're born there or have spent your entire life working with them, you can't be. I couldn't help a slight feeling of regret at being too old to fully live a Camargue life. On the other hand, had I done so I would have missed out on many valuable and exciting experiences forming the person I am today. I might not even have appreciated the value of the unique Camargue cosmos to the extent I did now. I thought of the chapel at the Laurents' ranch and the scene in the crypt of Sainte Sarah. Both demonstrated acceptance of life with all its ups and downs due to

Opposite: The well-tended grave of a famous bull: Le Sanglier died in 1933

AFICIONADOS !
ICI EST ENTERRÉ
LE SANGLIER
de la manade F. GRANON - COMBET
1916 - 1933

9·7·83
50ème Anniversaire
Club Taurin
LOU SANGLIER

Le Cocardier

CRÊPERIE   ⚓   CHAMBRES D'HÔTES

Farouk

a humble belief that we are not in control of everything, no matter how hard humanity tries. At sunset I came, as so often, to the conclusion that there is no need for regret. There is always a reason for everything.

Opposite: Bull art in Saintes-Maries-de-la-Mer

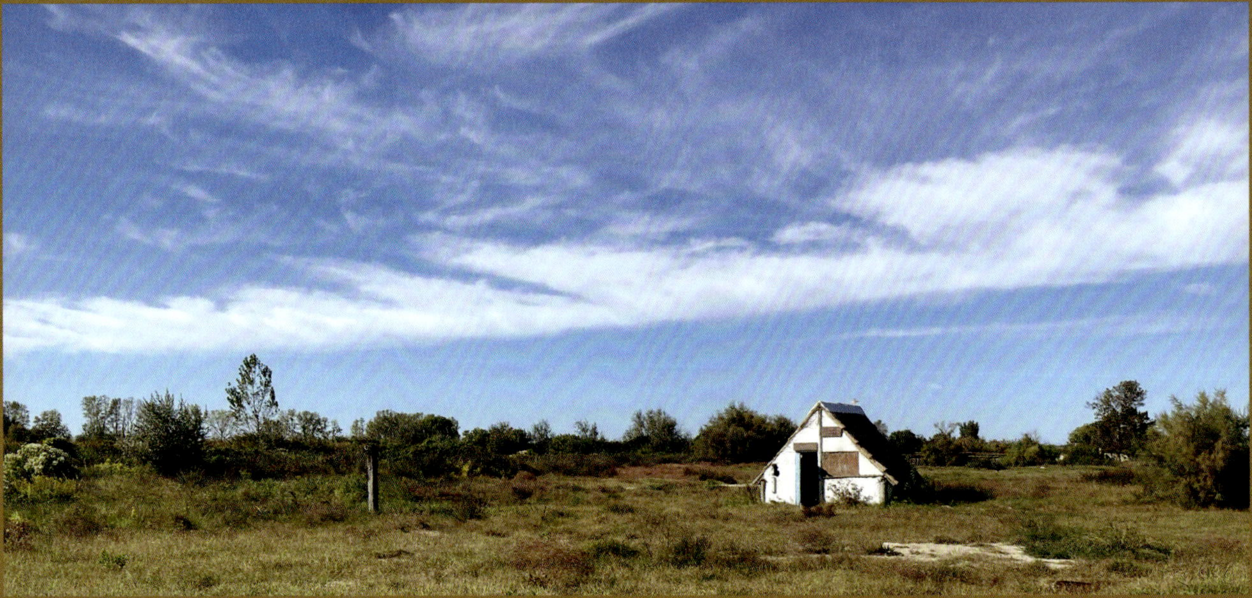

Chapter 5

The Stoicism of the Herdsman

Marlou was busy. Now twelve years old, he was at his peak. Like his famous uncle, Jupiter, he had the potential to win the coveted *Biòu d'Or*. He would have to beat five others qualifying for this supreme accolade. Unaware of any expectations, he did what he loved best – trying to squash all his opponents against the wall. Marlou was feared by every *raseteur* and some ran past him at a distance too far to ever touch his head. It worried us that he was too violent, sometimes damaging the cartilage of his chest bone when crashing into the barricades.

Every *manade* has sworn followers and for us *Laurentistas* these were heart-stopping moments. Our fear was not for the men but the animal, and one day the dreaded moment came. After a spectacular jump over six foot high he fell on his back. Caught in the narrow aisle between planks and wall, dazed and helpless, he struggled to stand up. People rushed towards him, distressing him even more. Henri and Patrick were sitting on the tribune reserved for *manadiers* and VIPs. Now I saw them on their feet, motionless, anxious. There was nothing they could do but their chief *gardian*, Nicolas, swung swiftly into action. Quickly but calmly he drove people away and then stood still, close to "his" bull. Slowly Marlou came round and managed to raise himself. Slightly shaking, he stood on all four legs – a good sign. Gently, Nicolas guided him back into the arena in order to re-enter the *toril* and back into the holding pen. Holding our breath we watched how he walked, how he held his head. Patrick stopped his competition, to the detriment of their reputation and that of Marlou – a few spectators whistled and booed because they couldn't see an obvious reason for retiring the bull before his fifteen minutes were up. Yet, Marlou's welfare was more important than any trophy. He seemed unhurt, but you never know until a day or two later if there is any strain, any tendon or vertebra problem. Thankfully there wasn't. Just to make sure, he was checked over by an osteopath once back home. This kind of accident and other mishaps can happen anywhere, even at home, as Camargue bulls are unpredictable; they may get into fights with each other, fancy jumping around or do silly things which only make sense to the animals themselves.

The main task of a *gardian*, a herdsman, is to watch over each and every member of his master's herd. Nicolas' performance, in a situation of panic and distress, had been perfect. It earned him the prize of "Best *Gardian*" on the day.

He stands in a tradition reaching back many hundreds of years. As mentioned above, though, his profession has not always enjoyed high regard and respect, with the lowest status lasting from the Middle Ages up to the end of the nineteenth century. In the past *gardians*

Nicolas, chief gardian at the Manade Laurent

worked in a Camargue that was very different from what we see today. The delta was truly wild; the Rhône and other rivers were largely untamed. Ever-changing water levels created precarious conditions for man and beast and yet, there had been farming since Roman and Greek times. The sandy soil on the fringes of the western Camargue was ideal for growing wine. Wheat and oats could be grown where the sweet water of the rivers dominated. Salt was harvested near the sea, at Salin de Giraud and at Aigues-Mortes, the only town in France with its medieval ramparts completely intact. The salt's earthy taste turned it into an early export hit. Salt and wine were shipped up the river Rhône or went abroad from the port of Marseille, founded by the Phoenicians. There were huge herds of sheep producing soft Merino wool. And, of course, there were the horses and the bulls.

This may sound like an agricultural heaven yielding rich pickings but it wasn't. Large chunks of soil were too salty or too poor to be farmed. Whoever owned land down there had to own a lot to make a living and the estates at the time, either owned by aristocrats or monks, were vast. The climate, very humid and oscillating between burning hot or freezing cold, didn't invite anybody to settle there unless they had to. Landowners and those who looked after the land usually left their families living in Arles, avoiding the mosquitos and the rough, disease-inducing climate.

The lowest of the low, those who looked after sheep, horses and bulls, must have been immune to any kind of illness. Like the animals, they lived outdoors most of the time, watching over their herds day and night. A *gardian* looking after bulls had his work cut out. Except for natural borders, like creeks and rivers, there were no fences separating properties until the middle of the twentieth century. The animals themselves decided where to go to find pasture and sometimes mixed with animals of a different owner. Any of the herd could drown during flooding or crash into thinly overgrown holes.

The *gardian* had to trust older and wiser bulls to avoid danger spots; they knew where to cross a river or find sheltered areas before a brewing storm unleashed its force. These scouts were called the *simbèu*. Many of them became famous for saving big herds from drowning and other dangers.

To this day the *simbèu* plays an important role. A herd doesn't respect him as an "alpha bull" but they trust him. In a way he is a double agent as he works for both parties – his brothers and sisters *and*

Securing bulls for a safe transit to a competition

the *gardian*. All *simbèu* wear a bell with an individual sound familiar to the herd. When it comes to separating animals from their group, the *simbèu* is rounded up first, hoping that the others will follow his example. When they go to competitions, the *simbèu* will be at their side like a trusted family member to give comfort and security in unfamiliar surroundings. Whenever a bull enjoys public attention so much that he doesn't want to leave the ring, a *simbèu* is sent in to coax him into re-entering the *toril*. It's delightful to sometimes see three or even four of them trying to retrieve their fame-seeking brother with all bells ringing.

In the past the herdsmen had horses but most preferred to work on foot to be closer to every one of their animals and spot injuries or

A lone Camargue rider

illness early. The *gardian* would use his horse mainly to get to and from work or to find an animal that had gone astray. Usually a long stick was sufficient to keep them all together – the bulls were either more peaceful in those days or they accepted the *gardian* as one of theirs. At night he would get them into one of the rickety enclosures dotted throughout the Camargue. He himself would sleep in a *cabane*, a primitive hut with one room, built from timber and mud with a thatched roof made from the ample supply of reeds in the Camargue. The rear of the structure, facing north, was rounded to withstand the *Mistral*, the icy violent wind coming down the Rhône valley. These *cabanes*, also used by shepherds and other workers, were not built for eternity but they have become one of the many symbols of the Camargue. Today renovated or newly built huts containing all mod cons are the most expensive holiday accommodation you can find to experience the "real Camargue", the swarms of mosquitos and flies included.

Our poor *gardian* of the Middle Ages had no luxury. He carried food for himself and his horse in a home-made bag. Cheese and oats, supplemented by catching the odd rabbit or fish, had to last for quite a few days which meant that the cheese, called *cacha*, had to be durable. Annie Laurent once offered me a taste of this cheese after a lunch, warning me to take only a tiny piece. My quarter spoonful had a strong flavour but seemed just very mature. Henri and Annie watched me closely to see how it went down. Two minutes later I felt as if my stomach walls were torn to shreds – this stuff was more powerful than drain cleaner! Yet it contained in a very concentrated form all the minerals and calories a herdsman would need to survive and it could probably kill any bug.

It must have been in those early days that the legendary reputation of the *gardian* was born. By necessity these men were completely self-sufficient, relying on their wits to make or fix bridles, repair their saddle, bull bells or any damage to the hut. They even carved their spoons. Most were illiterate but knew exactly how many animals they watched over and they had an excellent memory, enabling them to report any incidents in detail weeks after they had happened, to the *manadier*. Knowledge of herbs enabled them to cure the animals and themselves of illness. They created poems and stories of individual bulls and events which were orally transferred from one generation to another. Any spare time would be used to engrave horns, sometimes lost by the bulls, with delicacy and imagination. They wore what they could find to withstand rain and heat no matter what it looked like. For lack of means to buy a lasso they fabricated ropes called a *seden* by brushing out or cutting the manes and tails of their horses and weaving the strong hair into thick, twisted tresses. This could only be done in late autumn, when the assault of flies and mosquitoes subsided and no longer required a fully grown mane. It was a complicated and lengthy process but a hand-made *seden* was a precious possession lasting a lifetime. Today there are still two *gardians* who have this skill and there is hope that it might be passed on.

These are the traditions firing up a young *gardian* like Nicolas. I was eager to know more about him. By now I knew that there was a strong, rule-based ranking order in Camargue society. Before asking him to give me an interview I had to ask his employers for permission which the Laurents kindly granted before Nicolas agreed to give me some of his precious time. I thought he very much resembles the bulls he looks after: of medium height, he is all muscle. His eyes are alert and black like those of Jupiter. He moves in a slow, relaxed way yet always ready for action, like a curled spring.

When I met him, I was greeted by a sunny, welcoming smile. He wore a battered straw hat, a blue T-shirt and jeans as it was one of his agricultural days. Traditional gear is reserved for working with bulls or in public, but he had spent the very hot morning sitting on a tractor which allowed for cheaper, "civilian" clothes. We went to his office. There was only one problem: *gardians* don't talk very much, as if the silence of the wilderness they hardly ever left centuries ago had been printed into their genes. Nicolas didn't even come from a traditional bull ranch but, to begin with, he was as taciturn as his colleagues who had been born into the tradition.

I asked the obvious: 'What made you decide on a dangerous

profession which gives you a regular salary but has no regulated work hours?'

'Simple – I never wanted to do anything else. Becoming a *gardian* was my dream and I couldn't wait to finish school to find a *manade* to learn as much as I could.'

Nicolas hails from a local agricultural family and the pull of the bulls caught him when he was barely five years old. Later, he spent a brief period at another ranch to learn the basics before Patrick Laurent took him on.

'It's Henri who has taught me everything I know and I'm incredibly grateful for that,' he said with humble frankness and admiration for his employers.

Nicolas' day starts early. On a competition day one or more *cocardiers*, bulls that qualify for high ranking events, have to be separated from the herd. This can take hours as none of them want to leave pasture. Nicolas is chief *gardian* at the Laurents but he has the help of the family and amateur *gardians*, people with "normal" professions who choose to spend all their free time at their chosen *manade*.

Whenever I see them racing flat out to get hold of a chosen animal I can't help feeling jealous because of a strong desire to be part of it, but this is dangerous work requiring years of experience. Next, the reluctant beasts have to be coaxed into the truck that will transport them to the arena, sometimes over hundred kilometres away from home. The truck has compartments like a train and there are two bulls in each. Their heads need to be tied to metal tubes in an open roof so that they can't hurt each other while in transit. I've seen Nicolas and a nearly fully grown-up young Paul lying on their stomachs on planks while securing heads. It isn't easy: the slightest movement of a reluctant beast can break the *gardian*'s arm if caught between the horns. The next step is to attach the tassels and strings which is equally dangerous and fiddly but has to be done with total, absolute calmness. The only sound I heard was a soft sigh every now and then.

'Have you ever been hurt?'

He had to think for a moment and slowly shook his head.

'Not that I can remember,' he said. 'If I'm calm, the animals are calm. Well, mostly,' he grinned.

Once at the arena, they unload the bulls into a holding pen. *Gardians* from different ranches, although competing against each other, always help their colleagues before going off to lunch together. Nobody else is allowed into this illustrious circle. This is the only free time they have during the entire day. When the competition is under way, Nicolas has to make sure that his bull leaves the pen safely to enter the ring. Once out, Nicolas keeps a close eye on the animal. I have watched him many times during those fifteen minutes: seemingly relaxed, cracking jokes with his colleagues, I see that he is always totally alert and focussed. *Gardians* are known for their stoicism in the face of adversity but their hearts beat faster when it counts. Afterwards, in the evening, the whole procedure takes place in reverse. By the time the bulls are released home on the range, by the time a possibly malfunctioning truck is repaired and cleaned up, Nicolas returns home after a day's work that can last twenty hours. The next morning he's up again at dawn, seven days a week throughout most of the year. That includes agricultural work, repairing enclosures and gates in winter or any other tasks to be done.

'I love it all!' he stated with pride.

'Which is your favourite *cocardier*?'

'Marlou!' It came like a pistol shot.

He was my favourite too. 'Can you remember ever being in panic or any major problem?'

He paused for thought. 'Not really. But don't forget, I'm only twenty-five years old,' he protested at my eagerness to glean anything sensational.

True. He just looked much more mature and experienced and, according to Henri, he was one of the best of the fifty-six professional *gardians* in the Camargue. Probably he had experienced trouble and danger but saw it as a normal part of daily work. I wondered if he liked being labelled as the Wild West cowboy of the Camargue, a comparison found in nearly every tourist guide, but I didn't ask. He would have been too polite to say 'Not really' but it was obvious. His profession had a far wider range of responsibilities and a far longer history.

Like all professional and amateur *gardians*, Nicolas is a member of the *Confrérie des Gardians de Saint Georges*, a brotherhood founded in 1512 to guard against enrolment in the cavalry during times of war. Additionally, it has always acted as a mutual insurance and support cooperative at a time when a *gardian* had absolutely nothing to fall back on in case of accident or illness. This guild has given the *gardians* social status and a little security in times of need. It is the only surviving guild in Arles and enjoys immense admiration and pride. It also helps to encourage young people like Nicolas who live and breathe a life around bulls. I asked him if he thought that, in the age of social media, easy travel and a multitude of other distractions, the traditions could survive.

'Of course they can! They will. Nobody here can imagine a life without bulls and horses!'

The audience was over; Nicolas had to tend to the rice paddies. He slapped on his straw hat, shook my hand and left with a spring in his step.

Henri had shown me the purely agricultural side of their estate. They had forty hectares of rice which his father Paul had started growing in 1948. Wholegrain Camargue rice comes in a variety of colours and textures with a nutty, firm taste of a quality easily surpassing that of Asian production.

The Laurents had switched to organic farming early on. Henri had already shown me the intricate system of channels and pumps drawing water from the Rhône. On another excursion through their territory he explained how the pumps worked. They are governed by electronic sensors. Henri is visibly proud to be able to use modern technology to preserve old, ecologically friendlier ways of farming: the electronic pumps prevent wasting precious sweet water and crop rotation keeps the soil fresh, regenerating it without the need for chemical fertilisers. There is only one problem: flamingos. These big birds, so popular with tourists, often leave their lagoons to gorge on young rice sprouting in the paddies. Scarecrows are useless and farmers have taken to installing detonators to keep greedy flocks away. During my first year at the Domaine des Clos, I often woke at night thinking that poachers were on the prowl shooting innocent creatures outside the hunting season, but it was the sound of the detonators. I got used to them but so too did the birds!

The flexibility to use contemporary methods to preserve valuable traditions also applies to the *gardians*. Over the centuries they've had to constantly adapt to an ever-changing nature, to new methods of transportation and evolving technologies in agriculture. They may have lost some skills while acquiring others but they have certainly never lost their strong sense of identity.

The best opportunity to see the strength of this identity in action is to witness the *Fête des Gardians*, held annually on May

Preparing for the Fête des Gardians

Day in Arles and organised by the ancient guild. The first time I went I didn't know what to expect. Early in the morning, Arles was already tightly packed with locals and tourists. Hundreds of trucks transporting animals were parked on the fringe of town. I lingered a little, drawing in deep breaths of warm air filled with the familiar smell of horses and bulls, not appreciated by everyone. Next stop was the centre of town where more than 400 mounted *gardians* and *manadiers* in traditional dress filed down the grand Boulevard des Lices, following the ancient flag of Saint Georges, their patron saint. One of them is elected annually as *capitaine* who has the honour of carrying the flag. Amidst the sea of white horses and the black velvet jackets of their riders I recognised Patrick, Nicolas,

Henri's grandson Paul and a few others, visibly proud to be part of the exclusive fraternity.

Carefully controlling their mounts, they headed through narrow streets for the Church of Notre-Dame-de-la-Major, near the ancient arena. Once all riders were assembled in front of the church, the statue of Saint Georges was carried outside, followed by priests. The crowds fell silent. Even the noisiest of tourists calmed down witnessing a moving, powerful moment: the blessing of the horses. Religion still plays a big role in traditional Provençe but with a Camargue twist: this and other ceremonies blend animism into catholic ritual. It felt completely natural to me because we are part of nature and depend more on animals than they depend on us.

The church doors opened wide to allow entry for the long mass service. I stood at the back and over two hours I saw *gardians* darting in and out, dividing their attention between looking after their animals and taking part in what was clearly an important religious event to old and young alike.

Next it was on to the Place de la Republique where the Queen of Arles appeared on the balcony of the town hall. Applause erupted when she addressed the crowds below, dressed in the costume of the *Arlésiennes* and surrounded by her ladies in waiting. She is elected every three years by members of the brotherhood and, to me, seemed to play a purely decorative role. Later I would learn that there is much more to it, but for the moment I simply enjoyed the festive atmosphere, the colours and the sun shining over the most important day for the Camargue.

The afternoon was dedicated to spectacular displays of horsemanship in the arena. There must have been 8000 spectators and I sat crammed in, too far away to take any photos. Just as well because

A tiny Arlésienne and her rider entering the Roman Arena in Arles

it allowed me to concentrate on the skills of the Amazons riding in formation side-saddle, *gardians* racing neck-to-neck in the pursuit of snatching a scarf from the shoulder of a fellow *gardian*, or chasing a bunch of flowers defended by another to present it to "their" *Arlésienne*. The often dangerous games require extreme agility and control with horse and rider blending into one, like a centaur on steroids.

Even the smallest calf refuses to be dominated

Again and again I heard the name of Folco di Baroncelli. The mad Marquis had worked wonders to codify the Camargue culture. He had not invented it as some claim but he had unified it. Inspired by a meeting with Buffalo Bill who toured Europe with his Wild West Show at the beginning of the twentieth century, he worked to create the equivalent with the showmanship displayed on the day. Romantic as he was, he regarded the Camargue people as the last remnants of an indigenous culture like the Native American Indians and he stayed in contact with two Indian chiefs until the end of his life.

What we saw in the arena was a firework of breathtaking action in quick succession accompanied by symbol-laden ceremonies. Coming home late, my head swirled with impressions, images and sounds. Was all this staged for tourists? I wanted to know more, see how it all worked behind the scenes.

It was the gardener who helped me two years later, in 2021. Pierre looks after the Italianate park of the Domaine des Clos. Landscaping has been in his family for three generations. A big, burly Provençal from Tarascon with a captivating smile, he was intrigued to see a foreigner so passionate about the culture he was born into and which he ardently defended.

One morning he approached me, slightly shy. 'I have an invitation for you. I don't know if you like it or not. I can reserve a special seat for you for the *Fête des Gardians*.'

I was bowled over – what an opportunity! The Camargue had struggled through the second year of Covid. For over eighteen months bulls hadn't been able to run, tourists couldn't visit and the ranchers especially had suffered immense losses. After last year's cancellation, the Brotherhood was finally able to stage the *Fête des Gardians* in early June. Pierre spent a lot of his spare time as a volunteer, helping to organise this and other events, monitoring crowds and doing whatever else it takes to keep his culture alive.

On that special day he looked after me like a true *gardian*. Staying close to him while he worked with calm authority to keep the crowds in check during a multitude of parades, I caught a glimpse of the inner life of these festivities. This was a massive operation, a logistical nightmare at the best of times, let alone under the Covid restrictions still in place. It required hundreds of humans and animals to synchronise where and how to appear and do so to a strict timetable. Everyone had been up since dawn, loading horses and bulls, dressing up, driving their trucks to Arles, unloading, watering and feeding the beasts. I saw one *gardian* during a rare quiet minute gently caressing his horse. They looked into each other's eyes like lovers on honeymoon, in perfect harmony.

Pierre introduced me to the chivalrous secretary of the *Confrérie des Gardians de Saint Georges* who gave me top tickets for all events. That was an honour, but it was even more fascinating to explore the guts of the Roman arena with Pierre explaining in detail the maze of tunnels and hidden aisles.

'You can stay with me or take a prime seat close to the action,' he offered.

The Roman arena in Arles

I stayed with him, in the middle of the tunnel where gladiators once prepared to fight for their lives. Now there was the organised chaos of *Arlésiennes* putting the final touches to their attire, helping each other fasten bits and pieces of their beautiful but complicated dresses amidst riders checking their saddles, dusting their hats, brushing the manes and tails of their horses before entering the glare of the ring. It was a very hot day. Due to Covid the long mass took place in the arena and it seemed to take even longer than usual. For more than two hours horses and riders stood motionless in the burning sun, without revealing the slightest sign of exhaustion.

The games in the afternoon took place in front of less than 1000 people. There had been no time to advertise the event but that didn't dampen the enthusiasm for delivering excellent performances. Being in the tunnel, near the gate, allowed me to take shots at close range while overhearing all kinds of discussions concerning bulls, colleagues and horses. Pierre made sure I had water and a good view. Not only that, he entered the ring to pick up a bull's tassel, lost during a performance, to give it to me.

When I sat further up out in the open, an elderly Camargue lady squeezed past to take her seat, whispering '*Excusez moi, monsieur.*' As so often, I was taken for a male. Her eyes popped when Pierre picked up a lovely flower that had fallen on the arena's sand and nearly kneeled to present it to me. She breathed a sigh of relief when I told her I'm a female.

They pulled off the entire programme. It was past 8pm when Pierre was relieved of his duties and finally I could invite him for a beer. Sitting at a bar in the sun casting a warm glow over the ancient arena, we watched the last trucks leaving. For the *gardians* the day was not over yet. Anxiously, Pierre asked if I had enjoyed myself. I couldn't find enough words to thank him for the privilege of getting such a close look behind the scenes.

'You and all the others who worked so hard – you do it for yourselves, for the Camargue, don't you?'

'Of course,' he said, pride in his voice, 'and we'll always do it, with or without tourists and no matter what or how. It's our way of life. Of course it is!'

'Of course it is!' I reaffirmed with conviction.

Now we had a bond of shared passion. The next day I had a bottle of Bollinger ready for him and he was genuinely moved because he didn't expect a reward for supporting the passion of a fellow enthusiast.

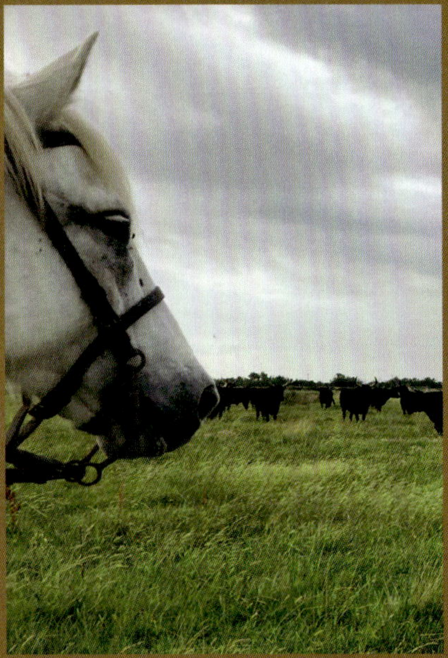

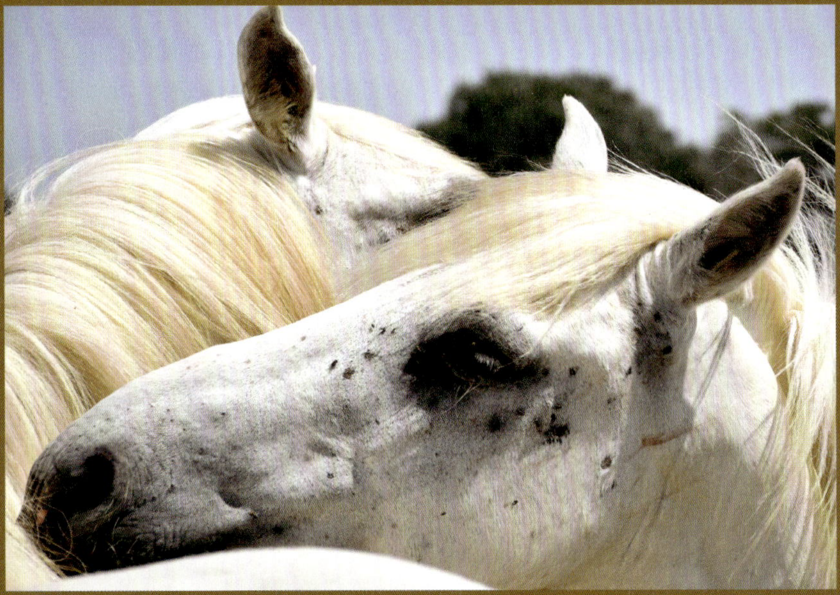

Chapter 6

The Camargue Horse – Your Friend and Colleague

With each precious visit to Les Marquises I learnt more. Annie and Henri gave me a lot of their time to teach me their way of life and to answer the hundreds of questions I had. Sometimes I learned simply by doing. One day we had just finished the bull patrol, finding all animals in good health with not a single one limping or injured by infighting. While telling me more about the sophisticated psychology of individual bulls and their interaction within their wider family, Henri steered the pick-up truck towards an area where some of their horses lived. There was a herd of sixteen, among them mares with their foals. He asked me to open the gate and shut it behind him.

'They will want to escape – make sure none of them get through!'

I was familiar with horses but I had never encountered the semi-wild Camargue variety at close range. Eager to comply, I prepared for the worst. Seeing us arriving, they turned towards us, ears pricked up. I opened the heavy wide gate for Henri to enter. Seven horses moved towards the exit I was trying to shut off as quickly as possible.

'They must not escape, they must not escape,' I thought, fearful of failure.

Making myself as big as possible, I began to shout and gesticulate like mad while jumping up and down to deter them. They stopped, unfazed but utterly bemused. Dark big eyes drilled into mine as if to say: 'You can't behave like this around here. We do have manners, you know!'

I came back to my senses, remembering my own, most important rule: stay calm whenever with animals. Quietly, I finished the task. Now surrounded by their warm bodies, I gently but firmly pushed back. Velvety nostrils breathed softly over my head and shoulders, then systematically proceeded to inspect the pockets of my jackets in search of anything attractive to eat. These horses were magnificent and so cool!

The Camargue horse is classified as prehistoric but nobody knows where they came from. Some scientists think that horses who lived near Solutré in Burgundy 20,000 years ago are the forefathers of the Camargue variety. A large number of skeletons found at the bottom of the rock of Solutré in 1866 were analysed and found to be nearly identical with those of the Camargue horse. There is no proof of a link between the two but the Rhône delta has been home to them for at least 10,000 years – they were there before humans arrived. Camargue people love legends and according to them the white horse crossed the Mediterranean together with the black bull in ancient times.

Like the bulls, they are fairly small due to the poor nutrition the Camargue soil offers. Rarely taller than 14.2 hands, they are true survival specialists, extremely hardy, agile and bright. Julius Cesar and Napoléon appreciated their endurance and pressed them into military service, but their true destiny has always been to help *gardians* with their work while remaining semi-wild and free. Since 1976 they have been recognised as a breed in their own right.

All the big ranches in the Camargue breed their own horses. Living outdoors all year round they would feel imprisoned if kept in stables and they are well equipped to resist Mother Nature's moods: strong legs carry a square, muscular frame. Thick, long manes cover neck and half the face to fend off the ubiquitous mosquitos and flies. Bushy tails are long enough to wipe most of the back clean of insects. Their hooves are quite broad to safely negotiate swampy ground. Yet what makes me really swoon over a Camargue horse is its head, squarely chiselled with an unbelievably soft nose and big eyes full of expression. There is a similarity to Berber and Andalusian horses and they may have mixed during centuries of Saracen invasion and close, not always peaceful, ties with Spain.

Watching the Laurent herd peacefully grazing in the sun always gives me an immense sense of inner peace. The foals stay close to their mothers. They are born with a dark coat and it takes more than four years to turn them into the brilliant white horses so popular with photographers from all corners of the world.

All the Laurents are totally dedicated to horse-breeding. Patrick follows in Folco di Baroncelli's footsteps with his enthusiasm for the admittedly much younger American horse and bull culture. The Camargue horse rests on a relatively small gene pool and Patrick introduced the American Quarter horse, equally suited to a *gardian's* work, to the Camargue. Inviting an "alien species" was met with much criticism from purist quarters. It has never disturbed Patrick's freewheeling spirit. His main interest is to secure a healthy future for these unique bulls and horses, even if this requires unorthodox methods.

One of the most famous horses in the entire region had been Henri's stallion, Esterel. I didn't know him but he must have been a miracle creature. The two were like a magic unity, bonded for life. Esterel was familiar with performing complicated dressage sequences at shows, sometimes far away, as well as more mundane tasks like rounding up bulls. He can be considered as the founding father of the present Laurent herd and when he died at the ripe old age of thirty-eight, the family was in mourning over the loss of "one of ours". Like many other beloved animals he is buried in the grounds of Les Marquises.

Annie Laurent in gentle conversation with a young horse

Whenever I returned to the Domaine after a day out in the wild, Sandrine and David, the hotel owners, wanted to know what had happened. They were not familiar with the neighbouring world of ranches. Bubbling over, I told them every detail of any new experience or event. As time went by, they introduced me to their friends in the area. These were well-educated urbanites, among them artists, academics and business people. Most of them were true intellectuals who had either come down from Paris to settle in the region or simply spend some time away from the fast-paced life in the big cities. I was offered a warm welcome and soon I had become part of this different circle, outside of the Camargue life. In a way they regarded me as an exotic, rare creature and it never ceased to puzzle them how a dual-national retired journalist from cool London could become so embroiled in the affairs of beasts with horns. They liked it.

Soon I was due for another lesson. One day in spring the Laurent ranch was bustling with activity: the farrier had arrived. *Gardians* and volunteers were busy assembling more than forty horses from pastures far and near in the yard. Camargue horses are not shoed because they live and work on soft ground. Their hooves are resistant to watery conditions that so often cause infections in the domesticated horses we know. I wondered why they needed a farrier.

'They want a pedicure at least twice a year,' Annie explained and sent me straight to work.

My task was to lead horses from the yard into the small stable next to the saddle room whenever the farrier had finished caring for an animal. It all looked like organised chaos but the atmosphere was calm. There was no chatting, no noise, no shouting. A *gardian* told me which horses to take in and in what order. Although I was a stranger, none of the animals resisted following me and sometimes I had two

Your friend and colleague

on a lead while negotiating several gates. The secret to their patient obedience was a portion of oats waiting to keep them happy while the farrier did his work. He checked their hooves for accidental cracks, abnormalities and parasites before filing off overgrown bits and giving them a final polish. In the distant past, wild herds had to walk endless miles to find food which prevented their hooves from overgrowing but modern times had changed their lifestyle which now incorporated more work though less distance to cover.

Apart from the odd tender whispering into a horse's ear hardly a word was spoken. Just in time for lunch we finished. The last horses, polished hooves shining in the sun, disappeared around the corner to resume their social life within their herd and I already missed the magic of being close to them.

I don't know how Annie does it but, in spite of the many tasks she fulfils in- and outdoors, she always manages to serve up a hearty four-course meal. The cosy dining area attached to the kitchen is reserved for informal family meals. Posters, pictures and awards decorate the walls. Hundreds of horse bits, some of them over a hundred years old, dangle from the ceiling. Their residence contains more artefacts than the Museum of the Camargue or the Provençal *Museon Arlaten* in Arles, founded by Frédéric Mistral.

Mealtime stands for animated talk switching between politics, art, philosophy and, of course, bulls and horses. The Laurents are seasoned travellers, having represented the Camargue culture in many countries around the globe but, except for attending a rugby match at Twickenham to witness France lose, they don't really know Great Britain, my home country for the last thirty years. To them it is an exotic island shrouded in fog ruled by a Queen whom they admire. Often they want to know more about British royalty, the ecological state of the Thames, the technicalities of the channel tunnel and the archaic customs of parliament. I usually answer as briefly as possible to gain time for firing a counter barrage of questions on all aspects of their life.

Horses – how do they train them? I was relieved to be told that the *Camarguais* are not "broken in". It would destroy their independent spirit and an animal fearing its owner would not be good at working with bulls which requires both horse and rider to act fast and intuitively. Every ranch has its own way to set out on the long road to success, but there is one thing they all have in common: patience.

That fluffy, cute foal looking at you already has a mind of its own and it will take a lot of gentle convincing to turn it into your friend and colleague. The best part of the first year is spent with its mother. She will introduce her offspring to the herd and the herd teaches the youngster all about hierarchy and how to socialise within the family. Every now and then mother and foal spend a short time in the stable so that the young one can get used to the presence of humans. As with the bulls, their first close contact with people is not a happy one but they all need to be branded when they are a year old. It's a nasty birthday present but the *gardians* have a way of proceeding as fast as possible. A rancher friend of mine, Laure Vadon, uses sedatives so the branding can be done with the horse standing upright and relaxed. That way they don't have to be forced to the ground and held down. She can do this because her herd is relatively small and there are only six or seven new arrivals each year. Bigger ranches can't afford this luxury because it would take too long and it costs a lot.

During the next two to three years the soft approach continues. Slowly they will get used to human touch. They will become familiar with wearing a halter, usually made of soft rope and they learn that being led away from the herd bears no danger. Eventually, they are more or less willing to train on a *longe*, a long rein which requires them to run circles around their trainer at slowly increasing distances. Every now and then a blanket is put on their back. Now their dark coat shows the first white strains.

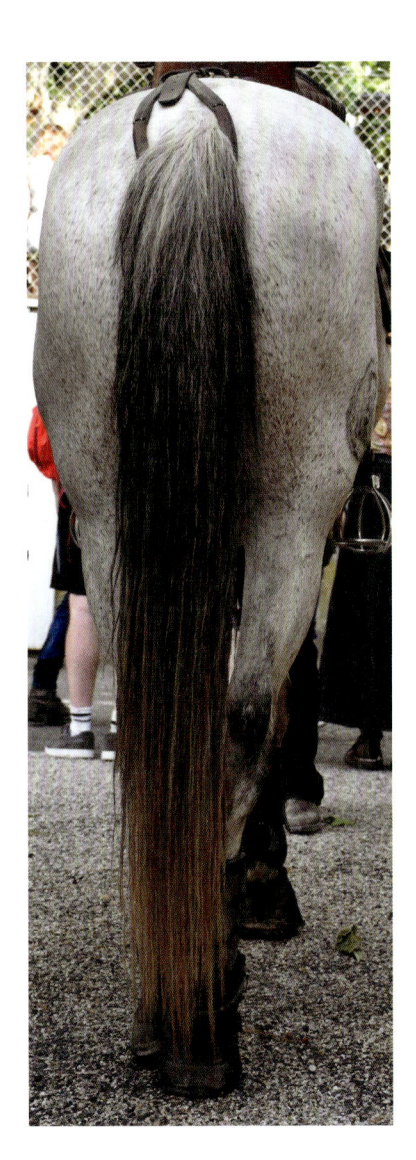

The fourth year is decisive. By now they are fully grown and it's time to familiarise them with carrying a saddle. The Camargue saddle, weighing fifteen kilos or more, represents a sudden heavy burden. Its design goes back to the Middle Ages when warring knights needed a saddle that offered enough support and comfort to "live" on a horse for extended periods of time. *Gardians* also spend a lot of time on horseback, but at least their mounts are not required to carry heavy and clonking iron armour on top of their riders. A good saddle takes up to a year to make. It costs between 3000 and 5000 Euros but will last for many decades.

The horse doesn't appreciate the expense and will initially try to get rid of this weighty nuisance. All training is based on rewards and little delicacies like carrots or apples and a lot of stroking will defeat the reluctance. To accept a rider will take more time and two *gardians* work in tandem to forge the beginning of a true working relationship. One holds the horse while the other just leans on its back to increase the weight. A while later he will get into the saddle helped by his colleague, well aware that he could be thrown off instantly.

The next stage is tricky. Bridles plus the elaborate bit and reins are added. The bit can hurt if handled the wrong way and it requires enormous sensitivity to teach a horse not only to accept all these strange things but to follow commands given by its rider's hands, legs and shifting body weight. I learned traditional dressage where the mantra was to maintain constant contact with the horse's mouth through the reins held in both hands. In the Camargue, however, they do it differently. Reins are held in one hand, usually the left, and most of the time they are slack, giving the horse space to make its own decisions. This can be a life-saver when a horse recognises quicker than its rider that there is danger. It can be a hole in the ground or it can be an attacking beast, but whatever it is the horse has to be able to turn away and accelerate at speed without hindrance.

Camargue horses and bulls have lived in harmony for aeons but a working horse needs to reconfigure its relationship with its black comrade. Instead of peacefully grazing alongside the bulls it is now required to herd or capture them. The bull will try to escape and that can also mean attacking the horse. Again it takes patience to teach a horse how to handle this task as safely as possible. The quickest way to achieve this is to allow the horses to see everything as a game with a reward waiting.

Eight to ten years after its birth the fluffy foal has developed into a gleaming white, highly skilled professional, capable of calmly but swiftly mastering any situation he or she is confronted with. They have become the perfect partner. The *gardian* can rely on the animal's intelligence and quick reactions – he doesn't have to spell out to his horse when to turn on a sixpence, when to back off from an attacking bull or when to accelerate to lightning speed to catch a zig-zagging, equally intelligent bull. There is no need to pull hard on the reins or violently use the spurs; a slight indication is enough. They have become one, acting instinctively and in harmony.

The pure joy of watching a pair in full flight is only surpassed by seeing them released back to their herd. I could marvel forever at noisy reunions after a long, hard day's work when the herd greets the returning family member with lots of neighing and jumping around followed by tender mane-nibbling. The Camargue horse can be your partner, friend and colleague but it remains wild at heart. You never really own them.

Today their future seems secure but that has not always been the case nor has their use been as varied as nowadays. Until the end of the nineteenth century their work was less than glamorous. They had to guide bulls into town, serve in the army or do farm work. When it came to harvesting, the latter was particularly tedious for *gardians* and horses alike. For weeks on end they were used as four-legged threshers. Walking in never-ending circles around their *gardians* from dawn until dusk they treaded garbs to separate the wheat from the chaff in intolerably dusty, hot conditions.

Henri Laurent's classic Camargue saddle

    Mechanisation brought an end to this practice but with it came new dangers to the Camargue. The number of horses declined. Monks and aristocrats had gradually sold their estates to businessmen whose sole intention was profit maximisation. Their plan was to drain the entire delta and turn it into a vast agro-industry dominated by chemicals. Artificial fertiliser was invented in 1903. Calcium nitrate, derived from nitric acid, enhanced crop yield and proved popular with farmers who, at the time, didn't know that ultimately it poisons both soil and water. Again it was Folco di Baroncelli who helped to save the Camargue by mobilising resistance and calling for the creation of a regional park, a dream that became reality eighty years later.

Today over 150 ranches of various sizes breed bulls. Their owners live and breathe the dream of winning the grand trophies. They still have to send animals to abattoirs for the simple reason that the amount of land you have governs the number of bulls and horses you can keep. Cramming them into ever smaller spaces would be against their nature; their original, wild character can only be preserved by giving them the vast expanse they need to be happy. Not all ranchers can afford to give the space required and some concentrate on meat production, although its popularity has grown only slowly. The meat is leaner than that of bison. In 1996 it helpfully received the coveted label AOC – *Appellation d'Origine Contrôlée*, normally used to promote high-quality wines and cheeses.

I remember a lunch with the Laurents where Annie had prepared the signature dish of the region, *Boeuf a la Gardiane*, a hearty and substantial meat stew with home-grown red rice. For a moment I stared at my full plate and so did Annie. She confessed that she would never be able to eat one of theirs. Meat sold at the butchers can be tracked back to the ranch it came from and she always made sure it was "somebody else's". Hypocrisy? To me it sounded more like a necessary compromise. Henri admitted that it was always difficult for them to decide who to send away and, although this sounds like a contradiction, it is one of the ways to guarantee the survival of an extraordinary species. Many bulls who don't fancy chasing *raseteurs* are still kept at home because they play a vital role in a herd's social structure.

Opposite: Lined up for a siesta

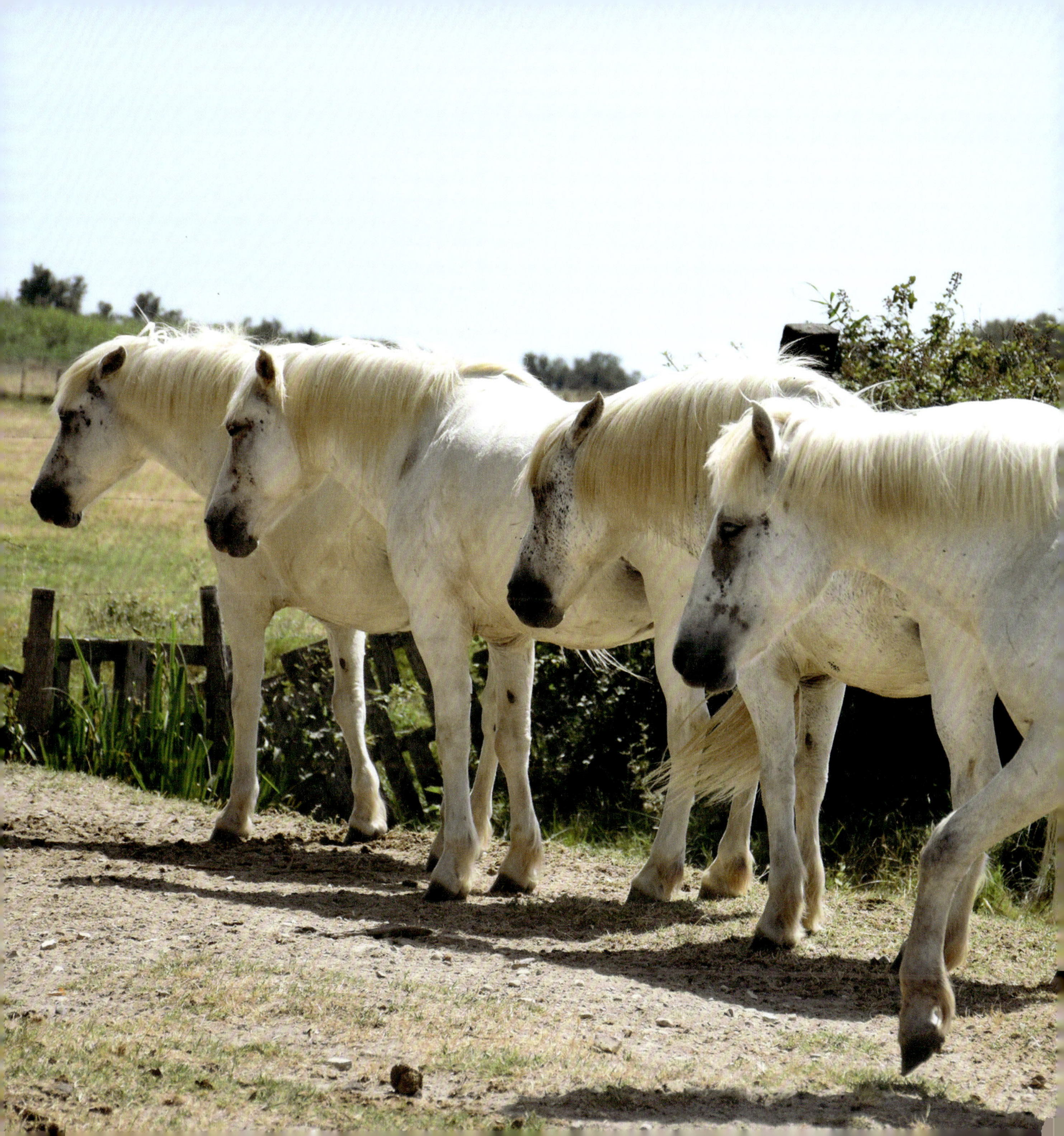

The rise of the *Course Camarguaise*, born out of teasing bulls in a farmyard, had given a new lease of life to the animals. The horses, now necessary to guard and round up the bulls, increased in numbers. Another one of their tasks was to accompany the bulls to and from the bullrings in the region. Getting the bulls to the arena always ended in a mad rush the moment they entered town. Any self-respecting male teenager would try to touch a bull, pull his tail or, even better, to separate him from the riders who were trying to get their precious stars safely into the ring instead of escaping into the streets or even entering shops. The arrival of comfortable trucks removed the necessity for this stressful experience which sapped the precious bulls' energies.

Camargue people love history and they love showmanship. Soon they found a way to keep the popular street spectacle alive without exhausting the stars: different bulls, those who are a little less aggressive than those who appear in an arena, would stage what is known as *Abrivado* (arrival) and *Bandido* (leaving). The fact that they are slightly calmer doesn't mean they're less dangerous.

Every town, every village has triangular traffic signs depicting a bull's head, warning of "bovine activity". The first time I saw one of those I didn't quite know what to expect. Would bulls appear next to me out of nowhere, sifting through the vegetables at the grocery stalls? It does happen but it is one of the more unpredictable incidents during a meticulously planned operation.

Saint-Rémy-de-Provençe is an elegant little town at the foot of the Alpilles hills. During the summer season bulls are as welcome as tourists. A run through narrow streets and along the boulevard requires traffic to be banned several hours before the event, high metal barriers to be erected and an army of security staff to enforce the now ubiquitous rules for health and safety.

On a warm day in spring, a waiting crowd was delighted to see all cautionary measures go out of the window once they appeared. "They" were a dozen riders in a tight triangle keeping half a dozen bulls in their midst while the whole formation galloped at breakneck speed through town. Several groups stormed past, hooves cluttering on the pavement accompanied by the 'Ho-ho' of the *gardians* who tried to keep control. The barriers proved useless; soon people were in the way, hanging on to horses and bull tails or worse, throwing flares to increase the mayhem, spooking the horses. A tourist, intending to get an up-front shot, was swept off his feet. A teenager, holding on to a bull's horns, had to let go and fell right underneath the stampeding herd trampling over him. Miraculously he was unhurt. I had somewhat mixed feelings about this raucous, accident-prone kind of event. How stressful was it for the animals?

Some ranches specialise in staging these spectacles. The two most prestigious ones are Aubanel and Lescot, both old Camargue dynasties. Annie's mother was a Lescot but Annie is not very fond of the practice of bull runs in the streets.

'One accident too many and we all suffer the legal consequences,' she says.

The Aubanels are legendary. Folco di Baroncelli left three daughters and one of them married Henri Aubanel who was determined to keep Baroncelli's heritage alive. A young Paul Laurent began to build up his herd in cooperation with Henri Aubanel and led Aubanel's bull Vovo to fame and glory. The two *manadiers* went their separate ways three years later in 1949 but they parted in peace. Just like Baroncelli himself, the Aubanels were not blessed with any business acumen and yet, Henri Aubanel and his son Pierre clung on to the way of life they loved. Like their ancestor, they turned out to be gifted poets. Like him, they risked everything for their animals,

They don't want to go home 'We are not going to leave the limelight!'

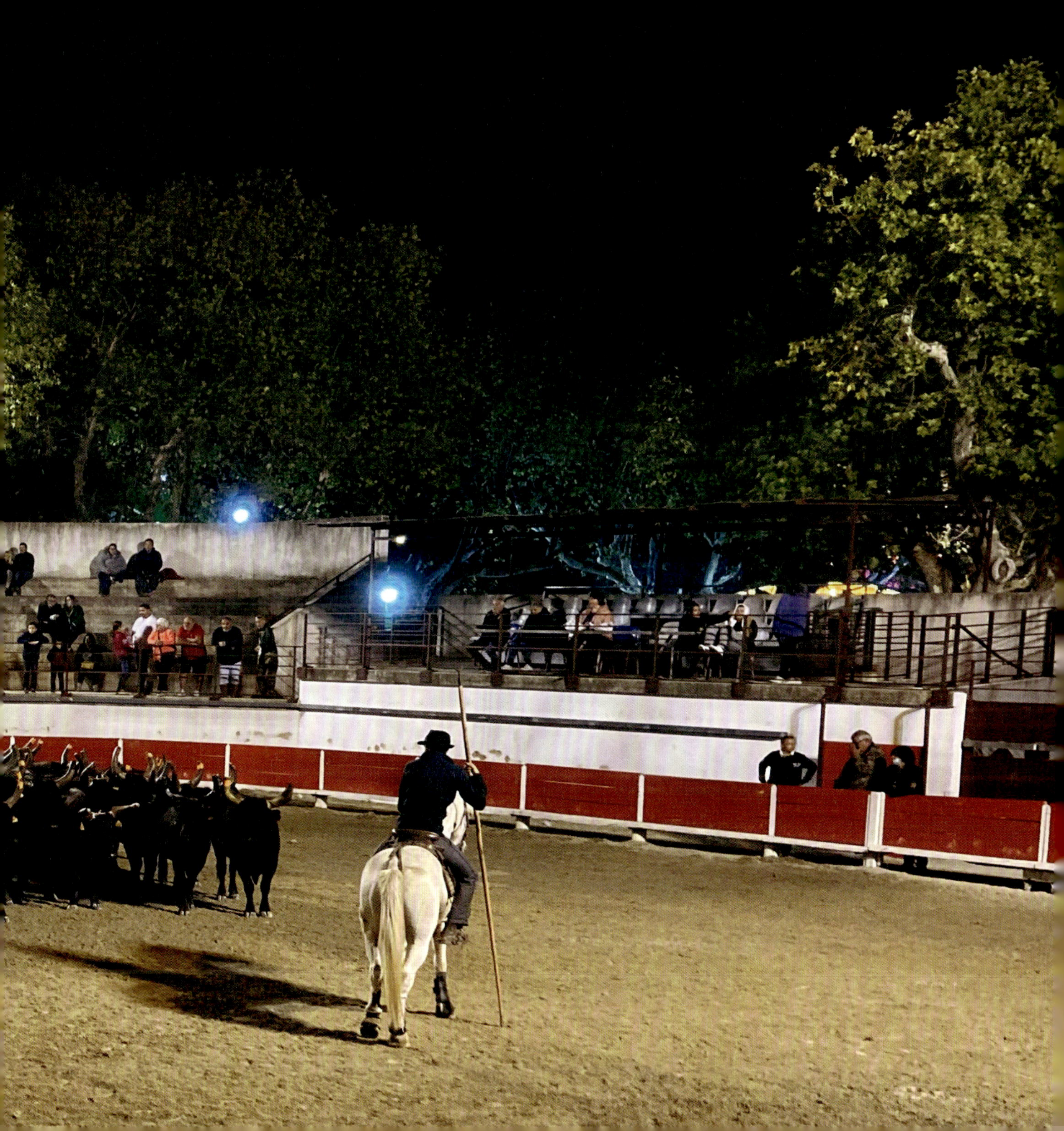

knowing well that 'there is no money in raising bulls' (Henri Aubanel).

Pierre, affectionately called Pierrot, died a few years ago. During the funeral procession his horse was led behind the coffin. The saddle was covered in black cloth and this horse would never be ridden again. Pierre's son Bérenger took over with as much dedication as his forefathers.

Specialising in staging bull runs guarantees a modest but reliable income. The animals are used to working in town; older beasts give the younger ones a sense of security and pass on experience. All horses wear ankle protection and they are shoed because they tread asphalt. They are not prone to panicking, no matter what inferno revolves around them, although accidents do happen.

Horses and saddles are elementary for this kind of business and an outcry of anger and disgust echoed through the entire Camargue when nine Aubanel saddles were stolen overnight. This is equal to stealing their livelihood and they had difficulty in carrying on working. The theft was especially painful as Folco di Baroncelli's saddle was among the loot. Miraculously, all of them turned up again a while later. Perhaps the thieves had realised that these distinct saddles were unsellable, that they might risk life and limb trying to do so. The long family trees of bulls and their owners have created a close interwoven community and, although normally competing, ranchers will stand together against any outside threat.

In mid-October 2021 there was an opportunity to see the Aubanels involved in a gigantic display of their skills. The small town of Bellegarde hosted the annual "110 bull run". In spite of the first autumn chills the streets were packed and the fairground next to the arena was bristling with lights and activities. Bérenger Aubanel and another rancher had combined forces to supply such a huge number of "streetwise" animals. Earlier in the day they had parked their trucks behind the arena. Unloading bulls and horses with a constant manoeuvring of vehicles and beasts looked like a logistical nightmare and there were delays but late in the afternoon, the first group of bulls was successfully released into the arena. From there they would run through the fairground and the streets of Bellegarde to a holding area, soon followed by the next group. The fairground was protected by barriers but the streets were not. I feared for the animals, never mind any spectators. Close to sunset the first group stormed out of the gates into town, led and followed by *gardians*. They gathered so much speed that nobody had a chance to get in their way. Five herds galloped past delighted crowds with the best to come: all 110 returned as one huge mass of shiny black bulls. Wrapped in clouds of dust it looked as if they were flying back into the arena. And there they stood, silhouetted against the dark night sky by the warm glow of stadium lights. Twelve *gardians* led by Bérenger Aubanel now faced the tricky endeavour to separate the bulls according to ownership and then get them through a fairly small gate back into their trucks.

The black mass had turned into 110 individuals with their own ideas on what to do next. Some were engaged in sorting out neighbourly disputes and clashed horns; thankfully these were covered in leather sheaths to prevent injuries. Several animals were scared of the dark gate and didn't want to go through. Others practised mating. None of them were interested in leaving the limelight; the smallest gap between the horses working in tight groups was used for escape and a chase around the sandy oval. By now it was seriously cold and, one by one, onlookers left until there were only five of us watching. Three hours later the last bull, heroically withstanding any attempt to get him out, finally had to give in to the combined force of twelve horses and their riders.

A night out in town

It was nearly 11pm. Half frozen I went back to my car. On the way I noticed an exhausted *gardian* caressing his equally tired horse. They had all been up since dawn and now they had to embark on a long drive home to release the animals back to freedom.

There are easier ways to make a living. This is the incarnation of limitless passion for nature, handed down over generations. Back home and tucked up in bed, I dozed off with the image of a thousand freedom-loving black bulls flying past…

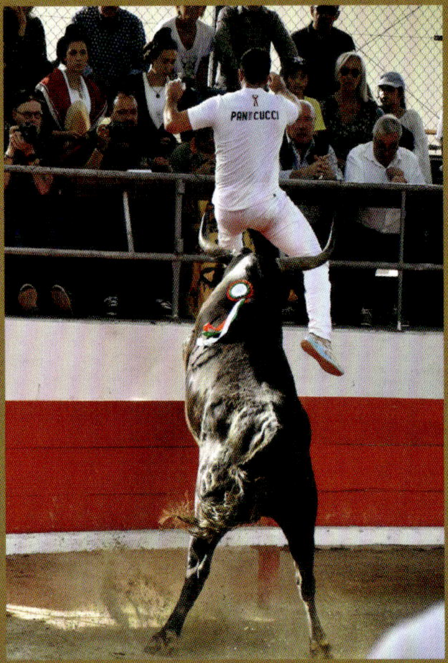

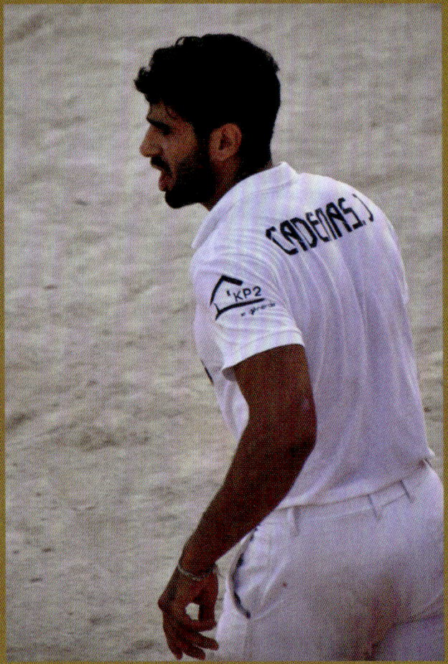
CADENAS.J
KP2

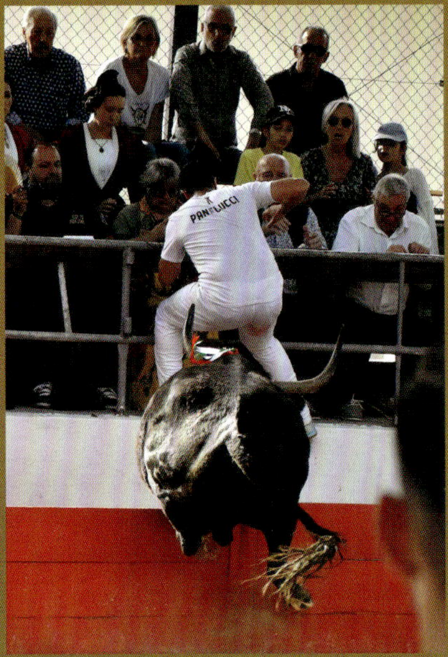

Chapter 7

Under the Black Bull's Hooves

Bulls "take" trophies too. Sitting in the arena of a small village, I watched one parading a shredded white T-shirt on his left horn. He was visibly pleased with himself. The young *raseteur* who had tried to pick one of the bull's tassels clung on to the top of the wall surrounding the ring. Bare-chested but unharmed, he breathed sighs of relief; only moments ago he had found himself under bull's hooves, trying to wriggle away from its sharp horns.

Going to *les courses* had become an integral part of my time spent in the Camargue. The season lasts from March until early November and there are over 800 *Courses Camarguaises* to choose from. Two to three times a week I drove off to watch Laurent bulls competing with others and, of course, defending the colours of their *manade*. More often than not, Henri, Patrick and Paul were there too, surrounded by other *Laurentistas* to support their animals. By now I was more familiar with the complicated set of rules and the system of points and leagues which had evolved over many decades. This also meant that I had lost the innocence of simply enjoying the spectacle. I watched the *raseteurs* with suspicion, critical of every run they attempted, every violation of rules putting the bull at a disadvantage or sapping his energies. I sighed when an iron claw came too close to the animal's eye, screamed in anger when two *raseteurs* attacked, against the rules, at the same time. I booed when they didn't engage at all for long, empty minutes. That I was totally biased, in favour of the bulls, would be an understatement.

What exactly is it we all want to see? What constitutes the perfect encounter between black and white? I choose to call it a *pas de deux*. This miraculous encounter happens when the *raseteur* starts off at the right point to meet the bull who knows exactly at which angle to meet his opponent. At this moment they begin to fly in tandem, the *raseteur's* hand resting on the animal's head until he has got hold of the tiny cotton piece he needs to take. When he does, the even more precarious seconds of separation result in a spectacular jump over the barricade with the bull, more often than not, following suit. This is what I had seen in the seventies with Goya. At the time *raseteurs* didn't have their names printed on their T-shirts but I do remember Patrick Castro, easy to recognise because of his enormous moustache. He and Goya seemed to have a special relationship with both knowing how to create the ultimate thrill. Many of my generation and older remember this period as the golden age.

Where had it all gone? I needed to remind myself that, in the glorious decade, I hadn't visited anywhere near the number of competitions I followed now, that we all like to glorify the past, that any tradition can go through peaks and troughs and that, above all, I had fallen for the Provençal custom of being very critical of pretty much everything. The artful encounter where man and beast bring out the best in each other still exists; it just doesn't happen every day.

There was another, more important reason for me to go to *les courses* and it was nothing less than supporting the survival of the Camargue itself. Bulls and horses are the foundation of this unique ecosystem. Without them we wouldn't see the unbelievable and rare variety of fauna and flora. Without them the entire food chain for hundreds of species would break down; without them the landscape would turn into a monoculture of dull, over-salted and muddy green, void of colourful birds and flowers. The productivity of the soil relies on the hooves of horses and bulls roaming freely over vast expanses, gently churning the ground. Their dietary preference for certain plants and herbs allows space for a multitude of wild flowers to flourish while the animal droppings act as fertilisers. The flowers attract insects and the insects attract birds, thus creating one of the richest bird migration sites in the world. The much-maligned mosquitos are an indispensable food source for birds and aquatic creatures. Heated discussions over spraying the insects out of existence or allowing them to maintain the balance of the food chain are ongoing. Of course they are a pain many tourists complain about, but without them the tourists wouldn't see what they have come to admire.

The *saladelle*, also called lavender of the sea, is the symbol flower of the Camargue. Between August and autumn you can see large, mauve carpets of it – but only where horses graze. Then there is a medium-sized white bird, a heron sub-species. The *héron-garde-boeuf* is often seen sitting on the back of horses or bulls, feeding on insects pestering the animals. It's a beautiful example of useful collaboration between animals large and small.

The black bulls are a protected species as fauna and flora of the Camargue are part of the UNESCO world heritage but there would be little incentive to keep them, or the horses, if it wasn't for *les courses*. It all hangs together and my regular attendance was a tiny contribution to the Camargue's survival.

For the games to be enjoyable, good *raseteurs* are required to bring out the best in the black beasts. Only this isn't always the case. But then – it's too easy to criticise anybody willing to take the bull by its horns. Opposite the main entrance to the Paul Laurent Arena in Beaucaire stands a memorial dedicated to all those *raseteurs* who lost their lives in pursuit of their passion. It was created by the sculptor Camille Soccorsi in 1991, the same artist whose statue of Goya dominates part of the town. Chiselled into a wall is a *raseteur* narrowly escaping a bull, the sole of his shoe precariously close to the animal's horns. The texture of the sole looks as if made of strings – it is the sole of an espadrille, the timeless cheap and cheerful footgear made of rope and cotton. Espadrilles don't offer much support but that's what young men of the past wore in the ring before Adidas and Nike conquered the world.

Next to the sculpture is a list of names, engraved in gold letters. The first recorded death was in 1881. The latest entry among the nearly twenty names was in 2020: Kevin Bruguiere tragically died right at the beginning of a very promising career. Every year in late spring veterans gather at the memorial to honour their fallen colleagues. They place gigantic flower bouquets as a reminder of the high price some have paid to keep a beloved tradition alive. Twenty fatalities over 140 years doesn't sound much, but this doesn't take into account the countless and sometimes life-changing injuries suffered each season.

So, why do they do it? Why do they risk life and limb to capture

It's a miracle that this raseteur survived unharmed

cotton pieces from the head of a wild animal clearly out to inflict devastating harm? Unlike a torero dressed in colourful and protective gear, a *raseteur* has no support from others weakening the bull and there is no ritual killing; the bull always wins. A French bullfighter wears white chinos – without a belt likely to be caught by a horn – and a simple white T-shirt. His "weapon" is the little iron claw (*crochet*) and its sole purpose is to snatch tassels while his true and only defences are athletic agility and anticipation. This is about passion, about history, fame and adoring girls. It's also about money because the sport has been professionalised in recent decades.

During each competition there is an interval during which the ring is sprayed with water to prevent slippage. Adults grab a drink at the bar and critically discuss what they've seen so far while the ring fills with kids playing *raseteur*, trying to emulate jumps over the barricades. At this stage their mothers don't yet have to worry about a dangerous pastime, but a few years on they may see their male offspring casting an envious eye at their older mates surrounded by a whole harem of admiring young women who wouldn't even think about entering the arena themselves. It all looks quite attractive and so they ask their parents for permission to enrol in an école *taurine*, a "bull school". Over three years they're taught by old hands, learn about the psychology of bulls, the culture of bulls and their owners and they learn the multiple techniques required to succeed in the arena. At the end of this apprenticeship they obtain a licence to compete in earnest. It doesn't always work out; not every veteran *raseteur* turns into a good teacher and quite a few students leave because they have underestimated the amount of work required and the dangers involved.

Patrick Laurent also attended a bull school and finished the course. He did so because he felt he couldn't criticise the performance of the *raseteurs* unless he knew their side of the coin. Very few ranchers, if any, have done this and miraculously he never got hurt, at least not in the arena. Young Paul, besides excelling at pretty much everything he touches, also enjoys confronting their young bulls every now and then. It gives him another opportunity to learn how to spot an animal's talent as early as possible.

The career of a bull lasts on average ten years, the same as the career of his human counterpart. The bull will retire to green pastures for the rest of his natural life. If he is very famous, he will receive regular visits from faithful fans. They are happy to watch him gorging on herbs while they exchange memories of his most riveting actions. He may even honour his visitors by looking straight into their cameras.

No such peaceful luck for a large number of *raseteurs* – in their mid-thirties they are no longer able to compete but the passion will not fade. It stays with them forever and they can't let go. Yet, there are many ways a veteran can stay close to the magical draw of the arena. Some turn to instructing; others become *tourneurs*, supporting their younger colleagues in the ring by trying to coax the bull into favourable positions. A few have established their own ranch, dreaming of raising the one animal that will win the *Biòu d'Or*. Then there is an online TV channel dedicated to *les courses*, always in need of commentators and analysts. A lot of them will continue to attend competitions, watching the following generations with a critical eye. Entry fees can be high and I wondered how they could afford tickets several times a week but then I was told that veterans have free entry and they will travel any distance to get their dose of thrills. It's like a drug and I'm addicted too. The only way to survive the winter-induced withdrawal is by watching videos of a glorious past and reading whatever I can lay my hands on.

Once the season starts up again you see familiar faces, like that

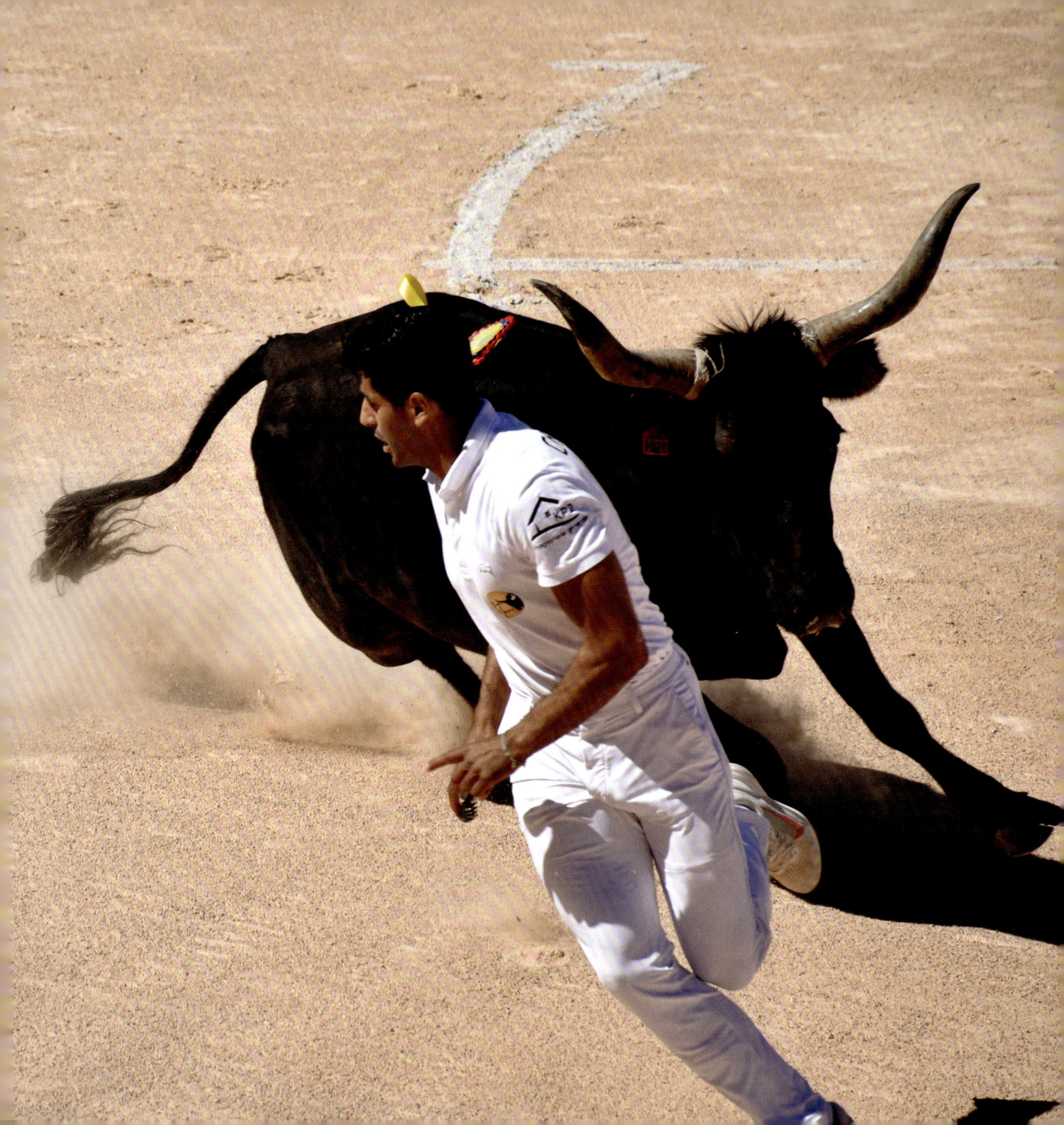

of veteran *raseteur* Jacky Simeon. He is easy to recognise by a silver-grey mane crowning a finely chiselled face. With his trim appearance and a lazy but fluid way of walking he looks younger than he is. Passion for bovine traditions is in the genes of the Simeon family and Jacky, together with six of his eight brothers, entered the arena in the eighties. Soon Jacky became a star – people loved his gentle charm and his ability to take on any bull, no matter how difficult, with stylish, flowing movement. When a bad shoulder injury required multiple operations, he didn't give up but trained himself to use his left hand to carry on.

All *raseteurs* suffer multiple accidents during their career but it is an absolute miracle that Jacky Simeon's name didn't end up in gold letters on the memorial wall for the fallen. In 1989 he took part in a competition that, once a year, allows an unlimited number of *raseteurs* in the arena, all of them desperate to win the *Cocarde d'Or* in Arles. Bulls chosen for this contest have to be mentally extremely stable to remain active and aggressive in the face of what looks, from their perspective, like a gigantic swarm of over-sized white mosquitos pestering them non-stop during fifteen long minutes.

Laurent's bull Vidocq was known to be extremely dangerous. Simeon had just made a run at him. With the furious black monster on his heels he tried to jump over the saving barricade but was hampered by a colleague in his way. Vidocq's horn penetrated Jacky's thigh, ripping open the main artery near the groin. Helpful hands dragged him, already close to losing consciousness, to safety. If it hadn't been for the fact that the arena of Arles has a small operation theatre, Simeon would have been dead within minutes. A fast-acting doctor managed to stem the incredible blood loss and give multiple transfusions before Simeon could be transported to a hospital for emergency surgery to

Opposite: The raseteur Cadenas escaping mighty horns

mend the artery and a multitude of internal injuries. It was one of the worst accidents in the history of the sport. The competition resumed after thirty minutes – the show must go on, always.

You would think that Jacky would never attempt to confront a bull again. Yet, many months later, there he was, back in an arena, greeted with a standing ovation by huge crowds. Sadly he soon had to realise that he couldn't perform any longer; the effect of the injuries was too grave. His career finished with a tour of farewells.

I tried to imagine what it feels like when, all of a sudden, in a split second, you are deprived of what you live for. What's the point of surviving when all that's left are memories and a huge void?

The same grit that had enabled him to carry on despite previous injuries before Vidocq put an end to his career, helped him to find a new purpose in life while staying close to the world of bulls. Jacky Simeon began to write. His first book dealt with his near-death experience, delivering a gripping and lively account of his adventures in the ring. Then he gave us a striking description of human and animal fate governed by the fallacies of the unpredictable nature they all had to live with – the beauty of a land they would never leave and the sudden devastation caused by torrential floods, drowning all living beings in its way. A novel was followed by an exhaustive dictionary covering all aspects of a culture centred on black bulls. Reading every single paragraph of this book gave me detailed information on terms and customs that a lot of local people themselves didn't have. His latest book has branched out into tourism with the unique idea to create a beautifully illustrated guide to all towns and villages in possession of a bull's statue and their connection to it.

Whenever I see Jacky Simeon, I greet him respectfully. Usually he answers with a bemused smile as he doesn't know who I am. He is said to be quite shy, which is why I have never asked him for an interview.

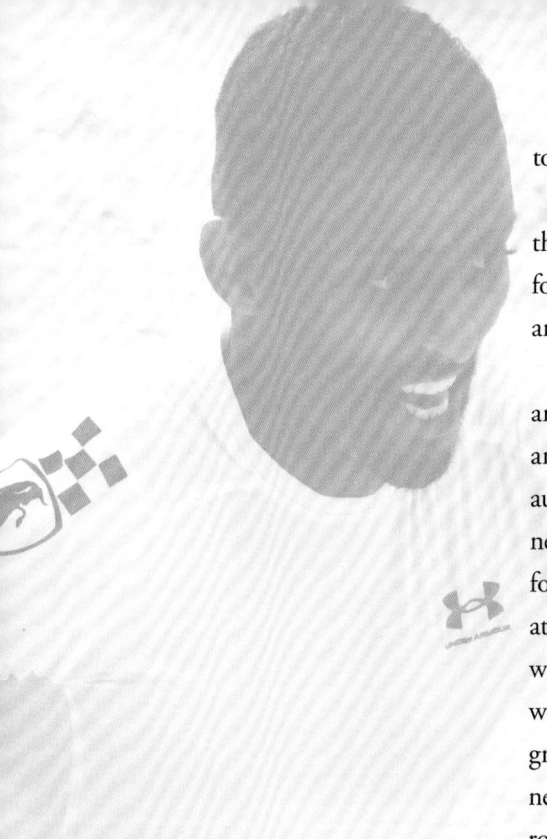

More often than not I hear the complaint: 'The bulls are not what they used to be!' after a less convincing performance in the arena, quickly followed by the counter argument: 'No, it's the *raseteurs*! They are lazy and they don't challenge the bulls! They have no respect for the bulls!'

Clearly the delicate and dangerous interaction between black and white has its ardent and competent critics. Most of these are at an advanced age. I had noticed the diminished presence of a younger audience. Internet, social media, and access to a wide choice of other new activities that hadn't existed in a simpler past, distract them from following the thrills of an ancient tradition which the oldies go on to attend with unwavering loyalty. I have to admire the tenacity of this wrinkly army defending their way of life. The necessity of crutches or wheelchairs cannot deter them from going to *les courses*. Others, with gnarly hands clutching sticks, umbrellas and cushions, laboriously negotiate the often uneven and steep steps leading to uncomfortable, rock-hard benches on which they sit down, relieved to have made it. No wonder they are frustrated when their expectations aren't met.

Henri confirmed that the bulls certainly hadn't changed their nature or temperament. As *manadiers*, he and Patrick would say that and I have to agree, having seen their formidable *cocardiers* in action and at close range at home. So, what has changed?

Another veteran *raseteur* had all the answers. Everywhere I went I saw a wiry figure arriving on a massive motorcycle at the arena. Equipped with fashionable sunglasses, a steel-brush moustache and usually in the midst of a crowd, Gérard Muscat seems always engaged in an animated discussion.

He lives and breathes the *Courses Camarguaises*, even decades after his retirement. It isn't easy to get hold of him as he disappears

Gérard Muscat following the action in the arena

seconds before the trumpet signals the end of the last competition, probably to beat the traffic. Eventually I managed to contact him and he was only too willing to give me some of his time. We arranged a meeting in the park of the hotel Domaine des Clos – it is near to where he lives and would guarantee an undisturbed conversation.

He turned up on the dot, armed with a large album of photos illustrating his career, offering me any I wanted to keep. Patiently he waited while I thumbed through stunning shots of gripping action, all taken by his brother who is a professional photographer.

'What made you take up such a dangerous sport?' I asked him.

'It was the cows. I was thirteen and they drove Camargue cows, horns protected, through the village. I couldn't resist trying to take them on. From then on I dreamed of becoming a *raseteur*.'

And so he did, for a long time without the knowledge of his parents. He didn't attend a bull school; naturally talented, he learned by doing, first appearing in smaller rings and eventually entering the "grand" arenas.

A captivating and eloquent talker, he effortlessly drew me into his world of victory and defeat. I noticed that he couldn't sit still; his gentle voice was accompanied by hands, arms and legs talking as well. He barely touched the array of nibbles on offer, eager to share his experience with an equally enthusiastic outsider.

In his first year, 1973, he ran without insurance – unthinkable in our age of health and safety. Every spare minute was dedicated to visiting and working on ranches, learning about bulls and their individual characters while training and competing. It can't have been easy because in those days all *raseteurs* held down a job. As a qualified plasterer Gérard worked from 5am until noon before he was off to a ranch or an arena, with or without lunch. During the seventies, quite a few of the big arenas were maintained and run by Henri's father, Paul Laurent, who also chose the *raseteurs* for each competition, organising the entire season in advance. There was no arguing who would appear where. Laurent's word was law. They each received the equivalent for 120 Euros to show up and they could win up to 600 Euros in prize money.

'For us this wasn't about money,' Gérard said. 'It was about passion and a way of life. The big change came when the *Course Camarguaise* was recognised as an official sport by the ministry of sport in 1993. They all became professionals and now there is a lot of money involved. And they train like Olympic athletes.'

That is something the bulls don't do and they don't care about money either.

Whenever a hobby turns into a professional sport, it offers a way to climb the social ladder. Provençc has always welcomed foreigners and I had seen a lot of *raseteurs* with foreign names. Some of these were extremely good at gigantic, showy leaps over the barricades and gained fame. But did they have roots in this bovine cult? Could they connect to this particular regional identity?

'Only a few,' he said. 'I can't blame them or anybody else who makes a career in, let's say, soccer. But bulls are not footballs,' he added ruefully.

I had also noticed that lot of the present crop of *raseteurs* didn't know the names of the animals they were confronted with, that they concentrated on the small red ribbon on the forehead of the bulls and the tassels near the ears. Held only by rubber bands, they were easier to pick and the *raseteurs* hesitated to have a go at the *ficelles*, the strings tied to the base of the bulls' horns. These strings don't come off easily and, while some manage to loosen them, the one athlete who flicks off the last bit of string is rewarded with the entire prize money.

'In my days it was different; we all cooperated in trying to get the strings off and we shared the prize money. That way you didn't have the long minutes of inactivity you see now.'

He explained that nowadays some of them get large sums just for showing up in the ring, which leads to risk-avoidance. 'It means the bulls are less challenged; they can't learn and develop their own skills. The result is frustration for those who pay to see a good performance from both parts but the season is long and the *raseteurs* don't want to get injured.'

If that was true, why did I see quite a lot of injuries?

'It's because there are more competitions than ever and they don't know the bulls well enough. They underestimate them. To study mentality and behaviour of bulls it helps to spend time at ranches and listen to the *manadiers*, but very few *raseteurs* do this nowadays.'

I asked him about his own injuries. His face lit up; gleefully he rolled out a whole list of battle wounds. He showed me a large discolouration on his arm where it had been sliced open by a hostile horn. He clearly wore his scars with pride. His face darkened again describing the one accident, a broken foot, which put an end to his career in 1989. He was thirty-seven and had already lasted much longer than most of his colleagues.

'I was devastated. For two years I couldn't go near an arena. Simply couldn't bear watching the others merrily carrying on.'

Gérard's body language said it all; remembering the ultimate defeat, he slumped in his seat only to straighten up again like a coiled spring when I asked him about his best memories.

'Oh, so many! I was so happy when my dad finally accepted my chosen hobby. And once I had to take on three bulls in the morning, and in the afternoon I took part in one of our biggest competitions, the *Palme d'Or*. I did well; afterwards we all went to restaurants and bars until six in the morning but the following afternoon I was confronted with Goya!'

He recalled his ultimate success: taking an accolade from Goya's head, 'a dream come true!' He remembered a duel with Christian Chomel, an equally legendary *raseteur* of the eighties, both racing to get the highest score, before rattling down a list of his favourite bulls.

So, what made him go back to watching the games in spite of all the frustration?

'I realised that I can't live without it. I go to any and all events. I can't give up hope for the future of our tradition and sometimes I encounter really talented teenagers, asking me for advice. I also love explaining what happens in the arena to interested tourists.'

The grand Finale du Trophée des As in Arles

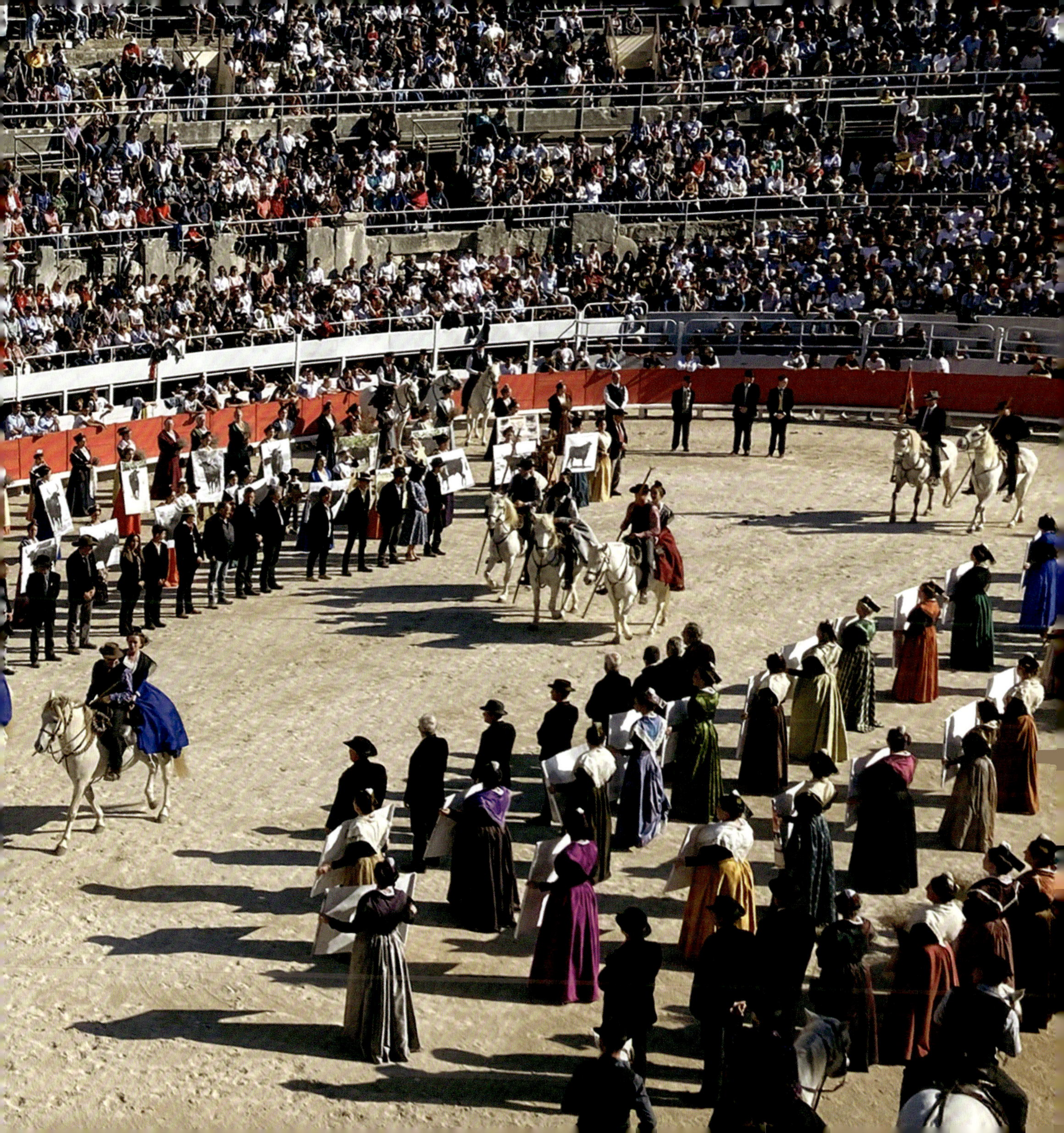

That was rare! I thought Gérard Muscat was an excellent campaigner for the Camargue.

And he was right: one should never give up hope. New talent would emerge. I liked watching Vincent Marignan, for example, whose entire family had been deeply involved in bovine culture for generations. His grandfather, Jean Marignan, had spent his life painting the Camargue and died the previous year. He had been one of the most popular painters and now it was nearly impossible to get hold of even a small drawing. Vincent, his grandson, was a dedicated *raseteur*, bringing out the best in the bulls and making every effort to please an eager audience – and himself.

In 2019 Covid had arrived, ravaging the entire area. Gastronomy and, above all, ranchers had to bear heavy losses due to the lack of tourists they relied on to keep the animals going. No *Course Camarguaise* could take place and that also meant that new generations of young bulls couldn't be tried and tested in small arenas. Life had come to a complete halt. Finally, in June 2021, the arenas were allowed to open again, under extremely strict sanitary rules. The famine was nearly over.

Competitions resumed and Marignan was tipped to win the *Trophée des As*, the highest accolade for the best *raseteur* of the year although it was by no means certain. This trophy and the *Biòu d'Or* crowning the best bull would be announced in October and celebrated with an enormous spectacle in the Roman arena of Arles, the grandest of all and Gérard couldn't wait to attend.

After waving him off, I was in a hurry to book the most expensive ticket one could buy when Pierre, the gardener, came along with a splendid offering.

'I'm on duty for security at the arena. If you buy just an ordinary ticket I'll make sure you get the best place for taking shots wherever you want.'

If it hadn't been for Covid I would have hugged him!

Not that Pierre himself was enthusiastic about *les courses*, not any more. Like so many he thought that the glory years would not come back and he preferred Spanish *Corrida* although he admitted that the *Corrida* too was in decline. Nevertheless he wondered why I didn't like it. We had a quiet and very reasonable discussion, similar to the one I'd had with Henri Laurent, about this very sensitive subject. I explained that I would never approve, let alone support, any kind of activity that hurt animals for the purpose of ritual or entertainment. That I hated dog and horse racing, not natural for these animals, for the same reason. Pierre had a counter argument, at least for the Iberian bulls destined for the *corrida*.

'Like the native black bulls they are important to maintain the ecological system. And they lead a pampered life in total freedom. I wonder – are you supporting one of these militant campaigns by so-called animal lovers who fight our tradition?' He looked seriously worried.

'No, I'm not. I have too much respect for your way of life. I just don't want to participate.'

We found common ground by agreeing that animal lovers would be wise to contemplate the fate of dairy cows and those raised for meat, mostly under horrible conditions. His mind was completely at rest when I told him that I'm not a vegan because that would mean the disappearance of all these animals and, in our specific case, the Camargue. It's simply a question of choosing meat as a treat and sourcing it wisely.

The big day arrived. Although the tourist season was near its end, thousands streamed towards the arena in Arles, filling more than half of its 15,000 seats. I was glad to see a high percentage of young people. From afar I recognised Gérard and other familiar faces. Annie Laurent rushed past at speed, greeting me quickly. She was looking for Henri to make sure he was ready for his appearance during the opening ceremony.

And what a ceremony it was! It began with the region's best orchestra and the traditional horse ballet. This was followed by seventy *Arlésiennes* entering in their silky costumes, solemnly unfolding seventy oversized photo panels – portraits of all bulls who had won the *Biòu d'Or* since its inauguration in 1951, the name and glory of each one commentated over the sound system. A long parade of riders and flag bearers lined up, representing *manadiers* and the ancient fraternity.

Then Henri entered, surrounded by a large group of small children – past and future united in the present moment. As they slowly walked through the centre of the arena, Henri's voice came over the loudspeakers. He had pre-recorded an emotional and unbelievably moving history of the *Biòu d'Or*, the beating heart of the *Courses Camarguaises*. You could hear a pin drop while he spoke. Handkerchiefs appeared and Pierre wiped his eyes as well. With the last of Henri's powerful words fading into the air, thousands rose to their feet, honouring the doyen of the Camargue.

Finally the actual bull games began. As the winners in both categories had already been chosen, we watched the *raseteurs* taking on the six bulls who had reached the final without the pressure to score points. They all made a true effort to perform with grace, elegance and respect for their four-legged opponents.

Thanks to Pierre I had a completely unobstructed view. He sat next to me and began to ask questions – his knowledge of *les courses* had become rusty. I gave him a running commentary on the action, explaining which way blacks and whites would move, when and why.

'How do you know all this?' he asked, slightly puzzled.

'Special relationship with bulls,' I said, 'and the teachings of Henri Laurent!'

Finally the trophies were awarded. For the first time in history the bull of a smaller ranch was awarded the ultimate crown and for Vincent Marignan a dream came true. He lifted his heavy trophy towards the sky, as if to say 'This is for you, Grandad!' Then he stormed up the ranks, hugging his father who had helped him to achieve the supreme goal. I bet Jean Marignan would have eternalised this moment in a wall-covering painting.

Once again we sat outside a bar in the shadow of the arena, its mighty walls cast in an orange glow. Pierre took a sip of his beer and, leaning back, he said: 'You know what – I think I'd like to go to *les courses* again. This was fantastic!'

My heart jumped. Job done.

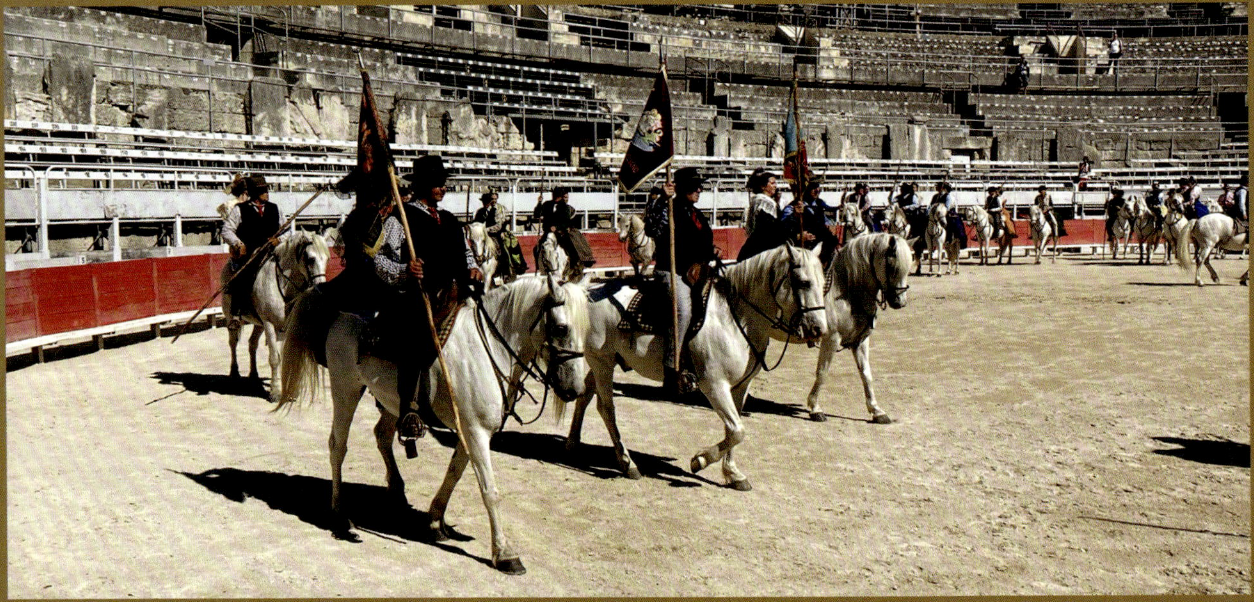

Chapter 8

The Loyalty Factor

At night the Camargue changes character. A dark, velvety sky covers the busy, noisy activity of nocturnal creatures like a comforting blanket. Sitting at 2am on the edge of the big lagoon, the Étang de Vaccarès, I watched out over the calm expanse of shallow water, listening to sounds whose source remained invisible. A slight feeling of spookiness crept up my spine. Had there really once been a haunted being, half man, half beast, living in the lagoon? Could there be one now, surfacing in stormy conditions when the lagoon turns into a cauldron of menacing waves churning the surface? Joseph d'Arbaud's novel *La Bête du Vaccarès*, written in 1926, described the heart-wrenching struggle of a tormented soul finally finding peace. The sudden shriek of an animal, be it bird or mammal, told me not to exclude anything. Our modern rational focus on the visible and the tangible denies the existence of another dimension, another reality, and I refused to be locked in by such a narrow view.

I would have liked to leave the hotel and stay for a few days and especially nights at the lagoon, completely immersed in the mysterious heart of the Camargue. Some of the big ranches nearby offered holiday accommodation but I couldn't stay with any of them as, a couple of years into my connection with the Laurents, the loyalty factor had kicked in. They didn't have cottages to rent and, in some kind of foresight, I had asked Annie if they would mind me staying at a *manade* not far from theirs.

'It would be awkward', she admitted. 'We trust you and we tell you things we wouldn't discuss with locals.'

Instead of being disappointed I felt a warm glow. To continue driving at night to get my other-worldly fix was a small price to pay in exchange for a deepening friendship!

Annie had simply applied an ancient unwritten law. The ranches were not hostile to each other but they were fierce rivals when it came to breeding the best bulls and horses. A *gardian* of one *manade* could meet up with his colleagues from other ranches – they often had to help each other anyway – but he would not have any meaningful communication with a *manadier* other than his own. If ever he left, he could not come back. The same law now applied to me and it felt like a gain, not a loss.

In spite of her diminutive size, Annie radiated power. Her clear, always sparkling eyes seemed capable of piercing the most defensive armour to find the truth behind any veiled attitude, no matter if it was based on shyness or plain dishonesty. She was clearly on an equal footing with Henri and the two were inseparable. It was up to her to decide who was allowed to enjoy the generous hospitality of Les

Marquises but she was just as competent doing the often dangerous work of a *gardian* even in her advanced years. This was rare in a society still dominated by males. More often than not she was out on a horse, separating recalcitrant bulls from their herd, mucking out after the horses or driving any of the sophisticated farm machinery. Yet she preferred to stay in the background, never claiming centre stage unless required by ceremonial duties.

Every year Mouries, her native village, stages the *Fête des Olives Vertes*. Mouries is located in the most picturesque part of Les Alpilles. Vineyards and olive groves cover gently rolling hills ending at the rocky cliffs of the medieval castle of Les Baux, one of the prime tourist attractions in France. In summer the scent of thyme and rosemary fills the air and to many this area is the epitome of Provençe. The green olives are said to be the best in the country and every September the forthcoming harvest is celebrated with a parade showing village life as it was 100 years ago. The locals pull out all the stops, dressing up in the ancient costumes of the baker, the candlestick maker or the shepherd and form a long procession together with their goats, sheep, dogs and rabbits while pushing carts full of local produce and old farming tools still ready for use, all accompanied by the local orchestra. The entire cavalcade is headed by a majestic horse-drawn carriage containing Annie and her prince consort, Henri. Gracefully they wave at a cheerful republican crowd hailing their Royals, tongue-in-cheek.

On the day, I was completely enthralled by this olde-worlde charm. Like a mad Jack Russell terrier I chased up and down the streets and around corners to see the carriage arriving again and again. Annie wore a priceless *Arlésienne* silk costume. I wondered how long it took to put it on and Annie admitted she spends hours to arrange the multiple layers in a flawless manner. I'm not that interested in fashion but

Annie's way of explaining this archetype of Provençal costume added to my understanding of her identity. She has a precious collection of these dresses, kept in a safe location and rarely on display. Some of them are from the eighteenth century. The origin of the costume goes back to the Middle Ages but its present form was fixed around 1900, allowing for subtle changes evolving with time. Christian Lacroix, a well-known fashion designer from Arles, sometimes visits Annie to gain inspirations rooted in Camargue tradition.

The *Arlésiennes* seem to be ubiquitous: present at every festivity and every bullfight. I often see them glide into the arenas, usually holding flowers and lining up in silence. Are they just decoration? Not quite. When it comes to tradition, Arles is ruled by royalty. Every three years a queen is elected to defend and promote traditions, especially the Provençal language. The idea goes back to Frédéric Mistral who, like Baroncelli, knew the power of symbolism and ritual. If people had a person to rally around, the common cause of preserving traditions could gain momentum. The first queen was elected in 1930 on Mistral's 100th birthday.

The criteria for candidacy are demanding: a future queen has to come from a family rooted in the community of Arles. The community of Arles has just over 50,000 inhabitants but its administration covers a vast area, right down to Saintes-Maries-de-la-Mer, making it the seventh largest city in France. The pool of candidates is further narrowed down by age; they have to be between eighteen and twenty-four years old on the day of their election, which takes place on the 1st of May, coinciding with the *Fête des Gardians*. They have to be totally fluent in Provençal and must have extensive knowledge of all aspects of history, literature and customs. They have to remain single for the duration of their reign. Last but not least, they have to be able

The Queen of Arles

to get into the complicated costume without assistance and, fully dressed, hold a dignified, stable posture when sitting behind a rider on a horse in full gallop. At least they don't have to be virgins but they must not fall pregnant. It happened once and that queen was swiftly and unceremoniously dethroned.

Throughout the last ninety-two years queens have been intelligent, dedicated young women, ready to give up any semblance of a private life for the duration of their reign. Together with their ladies-in-waiting they are present at each major ceremony, be it a traditional

Preparing to receive visitors

festival, the inauguration of an arts centre or an important bullfight. Each one of them has left a mark by concentrating on a particular aspect, especially of Camargue culture. Their speeches are powerful and their rallying cry is the glue that bonds this tiny world in defence of its unique way of life.

The present queen, Camille Hoteman, was elected in 2021. I sat on the Place de la Republique, squeezed in between hundreds of people waiting for the queen to appear on the balcony of the town hall. When she did, she was greeted by frenzied applause – for a day the French had turned monarchists again, relieved to be able to celebrate hope in the midst of the still rampant Covid pandemic.

Yet, in general, nearly all exciting activities, except for horse displays, involve male *raseteurs* and *gardians*. One could easily come to the conclusion that the Camargue is dominated by a macho culture. What happens if a woman tries to transgress the line into traditionally male territory? Is it possible at all? It is, but requires a trailblazer.

Antoinette Guillerme, better known as Fanfonne Guillerme, was born in 1895 in Paris. The family had roots in the western Camargue and long-awaited summers were spent at their substantial property in Aimargues, except for the month of August when stagnant waters boiling in the sun created a foul smell and millions of mosquitos darkened the sky. This August heat was said to induce pestilence and the family retreated to higher ground in the Cevennes.

The young Fanfonne soon turned out to be a tomboy. One of the first girls to attend a boys' school, she was used to male company. Dolls can't have been of interest but horses and any kind of animal certainly were. Her parents must have been enlightened, especially her mother Alice. Instead of confining her to needlework and piano lessons, they supported this inborn urge to live with nature and her very special talent: Fanfonne could communicate with animals in a way that would have Francis of Assisi pale with envy. There was a parrot that wouldn't let anybody near him except her. Horses fell for her gentle way of training. A young cow, saved from the butcher, became a pet in contradiction to everything that is known about bulls remaining untouchable. Bichette, as she was named, went in and out of the house even as an adult cow. One day, by now equipped with fully grown horns, she decided to innocently join a party of guests taking a stroll through the vineyards. Terrified, they ran for their lives, leaving the gentle, bemused Bichette calmly standing amid ripening grapes.

For Fanfonne, her menagerie wasn't enough. Soon she felt drawn to the rough world of *gardians*. The family had close ties with

Frédéric Mistral and his poetic movement of the *Félibrige*, with Folco di Baroncelli and the oldest established *manades* in the region like the Raynauds and Combets, all of whom had dedicated their lives to the preservation of the Camargue.

As a Parisian teenager she could have chosen the intellectual route to support the Camargue. Instead, she learned how to deal with young bulls in need of branding: first the animal has to be separated from the herd. Next, the rider has to drop down from his horse in full flight and, while still in the air, grab the bull's horns to force him to the ground. It can be a rib-crushing experience. She learned how to guide herds over long distances to and from towns or to seasonally different pastures, crossing rivers and swamps in blistering heat, frost and hail. She learned to withstand pain: when a panicking horse tore a rope out of her hands, the skin of her palms was ripped off. As if nothing had happened, she carried on working.

She also learned to live with loss. The western Camargue especially is prone to sudden flooding, when even small rivers turn into torrents and water comes up from underneath in seconds, out of nowhere. Valuable herds have been lost to nature's moods and *gardians* have died trying to save their master's animals from drowning. As so often, the loyalty factor came into play, overriding the basic survival instinct.

It was only a question of time for the Manade Guillerme to be born in 1920. Encouraged by her mother, she initially bred animals for the popular bull runs through towns and villages. Eventually she spotted potential winners among her herds and entered the world of competition. To find and nurture the bull capable of winning accolades requires an unbelievably fine instinct and soon nobody ever doubted this talent of hers. Supported by two faithful *gardians*,

Jacques and Armand Espelly, the Manade Guillerme became one of the most successful ranches, with two of her bulls winning the *Biòu d'Or* in 1968 and 1983.

Fanfonne never married. She had been engaged to a young officer who survived the First World War severely disabled. Not wanting to be a burden on her life, he cancelled the engagement. Fanfonne never looked at another man, focussing all her energy on nature and her animals. She promoted recognition of the Camargue horse as a breed in its own right. Ever practical, she also introduced the skirt-trouser outfit, allowing women to ride horses in the same way as men do instead of being confined to the one-sided Amazon saddle.

The year 1975 was the Year of the Woman and she went to Paris, nominated by the government as the first female ambassador of the Camargue. Was she a feminist? Somehow I believe she would have answered the question in the same way as Annie Laurent does: 'I have no time to even think about it!'

I wish I had met Fanfonne Guillerme. She died in 1989 and I have to rely on narratives of people who knew her. Robert Faure wrote a sensitive, moving biography of the young Parisian who became *la Grande Dame de la Camargue*.

Her charisma still resonates strongly. Every year the season officially opens at the beginning of March in Aimargues with festivities in her honour, including a grand parade through town, a mass, the blessing of the horses, bull runs and a competition of the most talented young bulls of the Manade Guillerme-Espelly in the arena. The Espellys, her trusted *gardians* and their children, have continued to guide the ranch.

Camargue legends are created by charismatic personalities and ultimately gender is less important than strength of character combined with a vision.

Still, Fanfonne Guillerme remains an exception. Personally I have never encountered open misogyny, but it exists. Some of it is rooted in the practicality of life: few women are strong enough to cope with the considerable physical demands of a *gardian's* work, but they are increasing in numbers. Although there is no law preventing a girl from becoming a *raseteur*, I've never seen one. I myself have often broken into male domains without any feminist intentions, just for the joy of the activity involved. Yet, even in my wildest, most athletic years it wouldn't have occurred to me to deliberately confront a Camargue bull. One simply has to admit that natural boundaries do exist.

The topic is more contentious when it comes to female ranchers. They are just as capable of running a ranch successfully and developing the instinct for breeding the best bull. The main obstacle seems to be men who have never left the Camargue and haven't noticed that the world has slightly evolved.

By pure chance I met a woman capable of moving heaven and earth in the Camargue. The Domaine des Clos welcomes guests from all over Europe and the US who enjoy the romantic setting. Some of them express interest in venturing out on horseback. There are umpteen ranches throughout the Camargue offering *promenade à cheval*. Since the 1970s the region has become more prosperous and the horses lined up for tourists are in much better shape than in the poorer past. The only problem is overcrowding. Long lines of riders with various levels of experience are led along the most popular trails, sometimes creating veritable traffic jams. A few hours of searching the Internet finally yielded a gem: the Mas Saint Germain, a ranch located in splendid isolation on the northern edge of the big lagoon, just half an hour away from the hotel.

The calm, friendly voice of Laure Vadon answered the phone and

Wild beauty in motion

only minutes into our conversation we quickly discovered common interests. When I visited the next day, I found myself in a time warp. The ranch was more like a hamlet, nestled between woodland, open pasture and the watery expanse of the Étang de Vaccarès. A main building dating back to the eighteenth century was surrounded by barns, stables, a riding arena, several sizable cottages and a pigeon tower. There were animals everywhere: bulls and horses grazed in surrounding fields; chickens, geese, a flock of six sheep, goats, two dogs and several cats freely roamed gardens and yards. Apart from modern farm machinery nothing seemed to have changed over the past few centuries.

Laure Vadon emerged from the saddle room, covered in dust. Tall and slim, she looked much younger than her mid-forties. Bespectacled inquisitive green eyes and a captivating smile greeted me with warmth. Over a cup of coffee – and a few cigarettes – we quickly exchanged

Freedom under wide skies at the Manade Laurent

life stories and were soon involved in discussing all things Camargue.

The Mas Saint Germain has been in the family for six generations. The ranch with its 200 hectares is well diversified: the Vadons grow organic rice and their own hay which costs a fortune if you have to buy it. Forty horses serve riders of all ages and levels of experience and some are sold to customers abroad on a very long waiting list. Others are carefully selected to work with the bulls. Each choice is made by all family members following engaged and emotional discussions. Five cottages welcome tourist families during the season and all guests are welcome to take part in farm activities if they wish. The solid business base enabled her father to realise his dream of raising bulls.

To hold it all together requires precise cooperation among all family members and, with three generations under the same roof,

*Rounding up
requires patience*

divergence of opinion can't always be avoided. While her dad and brother deal with bulls and crops, Laure and her mother take care of the cottages and the guests. Laure is also in charge of the horses, the riding school and the finances of the entire enterprise. She is well qualified to do so: she studied logistics and worked for several years in the UK, Spain and the USA. She had always planned to return and eventually an overwhelming longing for the open skies beat the perks of a successful management career. Her parents had never left the Camargue and it can't have been easy to introduce a modern, more efficient business approach precisely in order to save an ancient way of life.

Looking out over a sun-bathed prairie she said: 'You only appreciate what you have once you have left it behind. I have always loved the Camargue but didn't realise how truly homesick I would become while spending years abroad. This is my home; this is what feeds my soul and this is what I want to preserve for my children and all future generations.'

The perfect pas de deux

Laure has three children, ranging from very young to adolescent. Unfortunately her marriage didn't work out and she had to learn multitasking. While we were talking, the little one threw a tantrum. Then the riding instructor turned up to report a broken saddle. Next the thirty-eight-year-old arthritic donkey was nowhere to be found while a rescue dog, recently taken in, had killed a chicken. Without batting an eyelid, she dealt with each incident in turn.

'How do you do it? I'd have had a nervous breakdown by now,' I said.

'Oh, it's just the logistic obstacles of running a madhouse,' she said. 'I'm used to it. Love conquers any challenge.'

We had touched on dangers facing the Camargue and it turned out that she had recently started a movement to prevent the worst – harmful infrastructure projects, over-salinization of the big lagoon and pollution in the regional park. All on her own she had started to mobilise Camargue people who are not easily budged. I decided to join then and there to help out wherever possible. Laure was definitely a woman of power with a gentle soul. I left feeling as if I had known her for ages, and ever since we've stayed in close contact. The ranch is small and Laure is on friendly terms with the Laurents, hence I don't run into any problems concerning the loyalty factor by being close to both of them.

The hotel guests who go there for short or long rides in private, unspoiled nature, off the beaten track, all come back with glowing faces.

'We can't believe this still exists!' is an often-heard comment.

To a large extent the survival of the Camargue depends on soft tourism. The Laurents were among the first to organise weddings for celebrities or event days for corporates. Two long-stretched barns, formerly housing sheep, can accommodate several hundred dinner guests in either a relaxed or formal setting. Patrick and his wife Estelle love the USA and in recent years they have had a lot of success attracting American tourist groups who book ten-day luxury tours through France. Half a day at the Les Marquises is an integral part of their programme. Both Patrick and Estelle speak English and they continue to deliver high-class hospitality in Annie's footsteps. She is still very much involved but organising large events with cooks, waiters and orchestras has now become Estelle's task. Having studied law, she has a methodical and focussed approach to this second, successful career, one she might not have considered while at university. Marrying Patrick must have been a truly life-changing experience!

From spring to autumn, buses roll in and out nearly every day and the whole family go out of their way to create an unforgettable experience for their American guests, alongside looking after the rice and hay harvests, sending bulls to competitions and any other task connected to running a huge ranch, including the ever-growing modern burden of fiddly, over-complicated admin.

I felt torn between happiness about their success and slight resentment because I could rarely see Annie or Henri when the season was in full swing.

One day Annie rang and invited me to go out with them on horseback. 'Dress up as a *gardian*,' she said.

My shrieks of joy prompted one of the hotel chambermaids to knock on the door to see if I was all right. I left early the next morning, fully kitted out in *gardian* trousers, Camargue shirt, Camargue scarf and Camargue boots. There was a little bit of stage fright; I had never been on a Camargue horse and didn't know what to expect. On arrival, Annie presented me with a wide-brimmed black hat.

'It's yours to keep. You'll be part of our American show,' she said while making sure the hat had the right fit.

It got even better: I would ride her horse Voyou, an unbelievably rare gesture. She herself would ride Moise, her trusted steed for decades, now in retirement.

'A little bit of movement will do her good.' Annie calmed my worries.

A well-oiled operation was already under way. Groomed horses waited in the stable and a long trailer, equipped with microphone and sound system, was ready to receive fifty guests. The barn was decked out with tables and substantial snacks.

It was time to get into the saddle. Voyou, a ten-year-old gelding (a castrated male), looked at me with calm, inquisitive eyes. I promised him not be a clumsy burden on his back. Annie, Henri, Patrick and two more *gardians* were there. I wondered what I would have to do but

Annie told me to simply stay close to her, especially when it came to rounding up the bulls because they are totally unpredictable.

Our group of six riders stood still near the sheep barns with not a single hoof out of line. Annie did a dress check from hats to tails. Spotting my car key dangling from a belt loop she put it in a safe place. Saddles were adjusted. In a contest the Buckingham Palace Horse Guards would have certainly lost out on appearance and precision.

The bus rolled in and released fifty middle- to old-aged, excited tourists. Cameras clicked away for quarter of an hour before they all mounted the trailer, accompanied by Estelle, on duty as a tour guide, and with Theo, one of the farm hands, driving the tractor as gently as possible over uneven ground. If necessary, any of the Laurent family would have driven that tractor as well. Although enjoying the highly respected status of *manadiers*, all five of them were willing and capable to do the most mundane task subject to requirement.

The trailer headed to a spot in one of the vast fields while our first task was to present a herd of snow-white horses. That was the easy bit. Cameras rolled while Estelle gave explanations and answered a myriad of questions. Although she did this several times a week, she didn't follow a trodden tour guide routine but gave each guest the feeling of being special to her.

"Voyou" means bandit in French but there was nothing criminal in his behaviour. He made me feel at home on his back and his trot was butter-soft. I only had to think which way to move and he would do it. As instructed, I stuck closely to Annie when it came to fetching a herd of sixty bulls and placing them up in front of the trailer.

'Keep your distance and do not lose sight of any of them,' she warned me.

The animals don't mind contributing their bit of "work" but

one never knows. I noticed that there was a large gap between us and the next rider. As expected, a group of young bulls prepared to escape through the gap. Instinctively, without asking, I left Annie to direct Voyou in a wide arc to close the escape route and I was pleased to see the group retreating. For a while there was stillness. Patrick and two *gardians* demonstrated their skills. Focussed on the black herd, I didn't dare raise my eyes towards the fine, endless spring sky. Every now and then I cleared flies from Voyou's back. He liked it and turned his head towards me to have his face cleaned as well. This was a dream and I nearly missed Patrick's call for the grand finale: we had to drive both herds, bulls and horses, at full speed past the audience. The deep thunder of hundreds of hooves stirring up swirls of dust, with Voyou flying along like an angel, sent shivers of happiness through my entire body.

It was back to the barns for snacks and a tour of Patrick's collection of saddles from around the world. When the guests left, they said that this had been the highlight of their French trip so far.

The day was not finished. Annie and Henri had invited friends for lunch. During the aperitif Henri gave a little speech. Still lost in thought, I barely heard him calling me to come to him. He unrolled a document which said in Provençal that, from now on, I would be a *Gardian d'Honneur* of the Manade Laurent. It was a beautiful certificate created by Etienne Laget, a widely known Arles painter who had died nineteen years earlier. I looked at it, tears welling up. It was contagious; handkerchiefs appeared around the table. Once everybody had dried their eyes, we sat down for a three-hour lunch. Still in a daze, I could hardly eat. In the afternoon we were out in a pick-up truck to visit Jupiter and his brothers. Annie and I preferred to sit on the open loading surface under a surreal deep-blue sky. We picked

Every bull needs his beauty sleep

bunches of *saladelle*, which was in full bloom, and the day ended with all of us sitting outside under trees in front of the old barns, smoking and chatting while caressing two loveable dogs.

I left, not without Annie giving me more presents on top of the prized, now dust-covered hat: meat, home-grown fruits and a very old bottle of wine. I drove home very slowly, completely bowled over by emotion. Thankfully the roads were empty.

Of course I was not a fully qualified *gardian*; it takes a lifetime. This was more like receiving an honorary doctorate, but that didn't diminish its immense value to me. On the contrary.

I hooted with enthusiasm when Annie invited me back. On one occasion 150 American tourists arrived in three gigantic busses. After the show they stayed for a lunch consisting of five courses, accompanied by one of the best Gypsy orchestras in the region and waited upon by *Arlésiennes*. Even the Queen of Arles graced us with a visit on that day.

By now more confident, I mixed with people and answered loads of questions. One of "our" guests remarked on the quality of my English. Wow – I had made it! They thought I was a native and I felt like the most successful fraud in the world.

At the time of writing, nearly ten years have gone by since I rediscovered Goya, the miracle bull. For nearly ten years I have had the privilege of Annie and Henri's friendship and their teaching. My life has become dominated by the Camargue. It is time to tell their tale and the story of one of the most exotic, mysterious destinations on the planet, so near and yet so far for most people.

Opposite: As if he knows how attractive he is

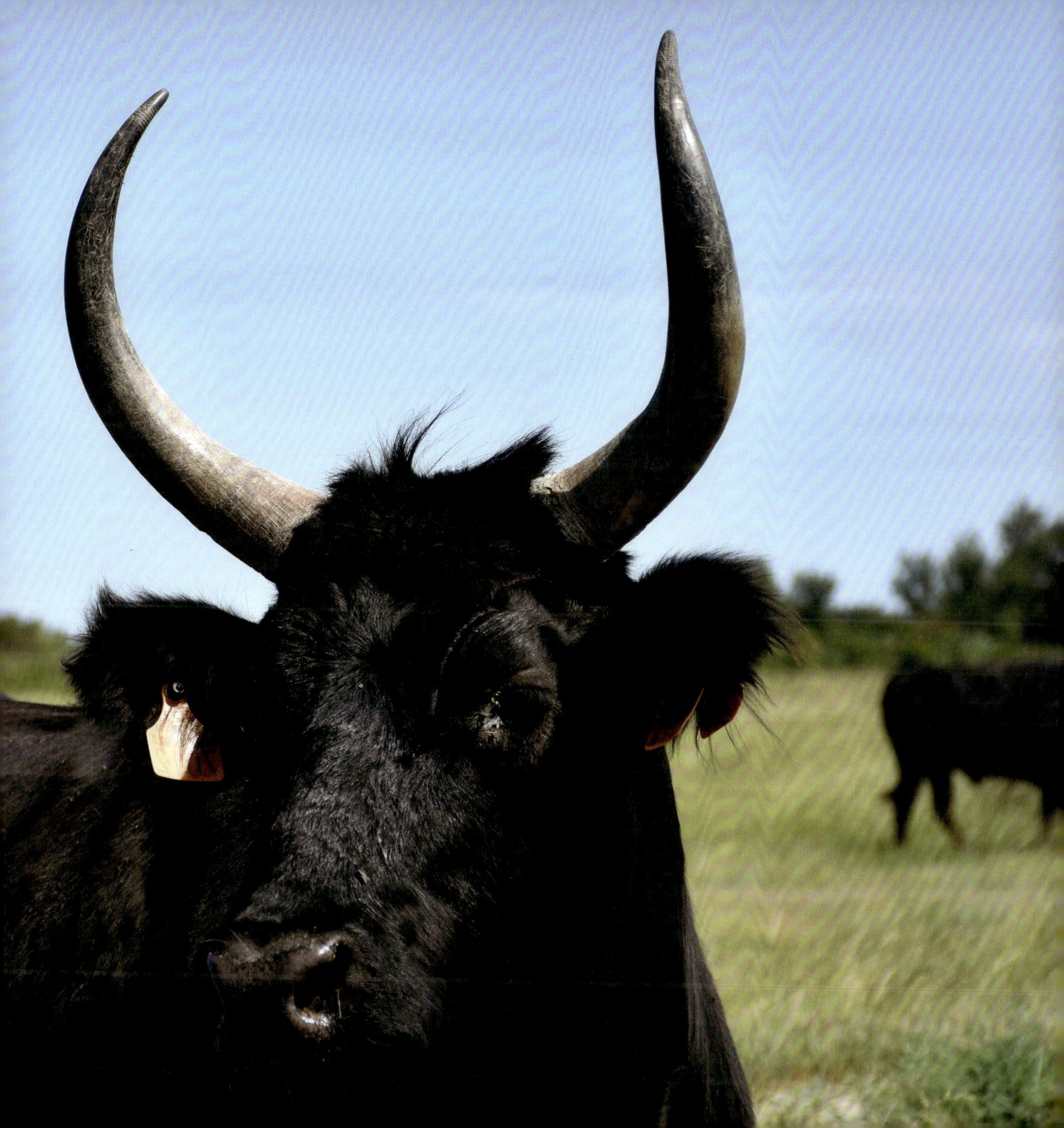

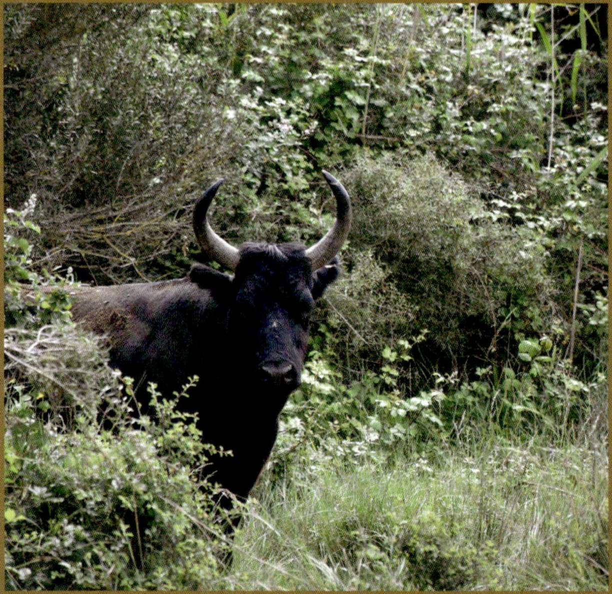
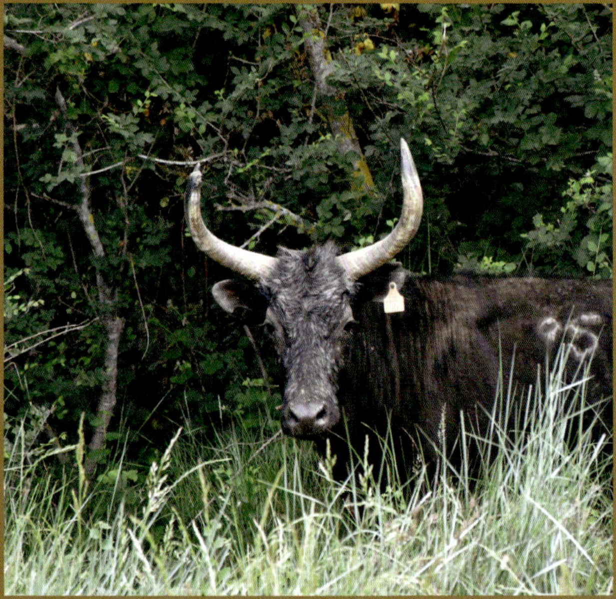

Epilogue

One day the sea will take the Camargue back into its embrace. Some say that this will happen in a hundred years' time. But how can they know? Time is a human concept and nature is not totally predictable. In the past 1000 years the ever-present threat of flooding has always been managed, somehow.

Meanwhile my journey through the mysterious land of magic black bulls continues; there is still so much to discover, so much to learn. Sometimes I have the opportunity to visit Jupiter in his retirement home, located in a separate part of the Laurent kingdom. Fifty hectares of secluded dense, shady woodland and rich open pasture are reserved for their best animals, nurturing those who still compete and rewarding others whose career has ended.

Jupiter has become quite shy and it takes a while to find him in

Sunset in the Camargue

a wilderness that hasn't changed in centuries. He is seventeen now, yet still dominates the small herd around him, including his nephew Marlou. The once foul-mooded, violent teenager has grown into a grey-haired elderly gentleman. They may live for a long time to come. They may die in their sleep or be killed off by younger relatives keen to claim the crown of dominance – we don't know. To separate fragile animals from their families and pen them into a "safe" enclosure would be cruel. Nature will take its own course, as it has done since the dawn of light.

Real danger to the Camargue is far more imminent than climate change. This danger is related to human enthusiasm for unwieldy, unnatural projects of infrastructure. The Camargue community is small and widely scattered over the vast expanse of the Rhône delta. Their pace of life is slow and it requires the energy of enlightened local souls with foresight to alert us, let alone unite this mix of individualistic eccentrics. I have joined initiatives trying to prevent the destruction of the last coastal wilderness in Europe. If tribal identity prevails, we will succeed.

I hope you, dear reader, have enjoyed my glimpse into a different universe close to and yet remote from the all-consuming rat race of modern civilisation. Nowhere can you be closer to nature than in the Camargue in all its beauty and all its roughness.

Those who feel attracted to following its fate can find more information on **www.blackbullmagic.com**.

© **Maritta Kaumanns 2023**

Appendix

Musée de la Camargue

This rural museum near Arles is integrated into the working agricultural estate of the Mas Rousty. It covers all aspects of Camargue life in a simple and visually attractive fashion, with changing exhibitions and topical events. The large sign-posted outdoor trail is never overcrowded.

Museon Arlaten, Arles

www.museonarlaten.fr/en

Founded by Frédéric Mistral in 1899, the museum is dedicated to the history and culture of Provence. The building itself reflects 2000 years of architecture in Arles. After 11 years of renovation, the museum re-opened in 2021 with a wealth of user-friendly technology, displaying its 3600 objects in a modern context while taking the visitor on a spectacular journey through time.

Parc Ornithologique du Pont de Gau

www.parcornithologique.com

The park covers 60 hectares of marshland near Saintes-Maries-de-la-Mer and is dedicated to the discovery and protection of Camargue Nature. Little islands and woodlands offer a peaceful atmosphere. More than 4 miles of sign-posted nature trails vary in lengths. You can watch a plethora of wildlife, with a guaranteed opportunity to take close-up shots of Flamingos and all other animals.

Mas Saint Germain

en.massaintgermain.com

Located on the northern end of the biggest lagoon in the Camargue and close to Arles, this traditional farm on 200 hectares with a wealth of animals invites you to enjoy a holiday in unspoilt nature. The Mas Saint Germain has been in the family for six generations, dedicated to growing organic crops and protecting the environment. Comfortable accommodation consists of five modernised historical cottages and two large rooms. They offer excursions on horseback on the vast private grounds, riding lessons, the opportunity to take part in rounding up bulls and other rural activities. The atmosphere is warm-hearted and the pace of life is slow – the perfect antidote to the modern rat-race.

Domaine des Clos, Beaucaire

www.domaine-des-clos.com

For those who want the best of both worlds, the secluded historic winery offers high-class accommodation in the midst of an Italianate park, surrounded by olive groves. The location is ideal for those who want to explore the best attractions of Provence – Arles, Nimes, Saint Remy de Provence, the Pont du Gard and Les Baux are only a short distance away, as is the Camargue. The hotel with its spacious rooms, suites and apartments received a four-star rating, yet the owners have maintained the friendly atmosphere of a private, welcoming home for their guests.

Manade Laurent

www.manadelaurent.com

Les Marquises, situated in the heart of the Camargue, is the legendary home to some of the most famous bulls the region has ever seen. The vast estate does not offer accommodation but the Laurents host tourist groups to witness spectacular displays of horsemanship with an entertaining insight into real Camargue life. They also organise large events for corporate clients and lavish weddings in romantic settings no couple will ever forget.

Sources

Most books on the Camargue are written in French and directed at an insider audience. I have selected and listed a few below out of hundreds of publications:

D'Arbaud, Joseph, *La Bête du Vaccarès,* Librairie Grasset 1926

Chevalier, Annelyse, *Les Gardians de Camargue,* Courrier du Parc no 56, 2007

L'Encyclopédie de la Camargue, Libella, Paris 2013

Faure, Robert, *En Camargue avec Fanfonne Guillerme*, Nouvelles Presses du Languedoc 2008

Migoule, Serge, *Folco de Baroncelli – Lou* Marqués, Éditions de la Fenestrelle 2017

Naudot, Carle, *Camargue et Gardians*, Actes Sud 2011 (originally 1945)

Pont, Gérard, *Goya – Seigneur de Camargue*, Éditions le Camariguo, Nimes 1981

Simeon, Jacky, *Dictionnaire de la Course Camarguaise*, Éditions Au Diable Vauvert 2020

All other books written by Simeon.

Valade, J Daniel, *Un siècle d'avenir en Camargue – La Manade Laurent*, Imprimerie Notre Dame, Nimes 1990

Other sources:

A website listing all competitions, including the names of bulls and raseteurs: *www.ffcc.info/le_calendrier_des_courses*

The website **Bouvine et Traditions**: *www.bouvine.info*

The Internet TV channel *Le Toril*.